STUDIES IN COMPARATIVE LITERATURE

EDITED BY

MOHIT K. RAY

ATLANTIC

PUBLISHERS & DISTRIBUTORS (P) LTD

Published by
ATLANTIC
PUBLISHERS & DISTRIBUTORS (P) LTD
7/22, Ansari Road, Darya Ganj, New Delhi-110002
Phones : +91-11-40775252, 40775214, 23273880, 23275880
Fax: +91-11-23285873
Web: www.atlanticbooks.com
E-mail: orders@atlanticbooks.com

Printed & bound in India by Atlantic Print Services

PREFACE

Comparative Literature is, in essence, comparative criticism and is as old as literary criticism itself, because comparison and analysis have been and continue to be the principal tools of literary criticism since Aristotle. Of the early practitioners Quintilian and Longinus tried the comparative method fairly systematically. However, Comparative Literature as an independent discipline is, comparatively, a recent phenomenon. Historically, the term "Comparative Literature" is said to have been first used by H.M. Posnett in 1886. But he used the term not exactly in the sense it is used now. The origin of "Comparative Literature" in the modern context must be attributed to Matthew Arnold who was a relentless advocate and practitioner of Comparative Literature. The contemporary intellectual climate is in favour of the opinion that while the goodness of a literary work can be judged by absolute criteria its greatness or otherwise cannot be judged unless it is compared with other literary works. The final evaluation must be relative.

The present volume offers a collection of such critical evaluations of literary texts by scholars who have applied the insights of Comparative Literature in order to bring out/ underscore the subtle suggestions and profound meanings of the texts so compared.

Amarnath Jha in his scholarly article brilliantly maps out the influence of Sanskrit grammar on the development of modern linguistics.

Asha Choubey tries to establish with fine literary sensibility how Bharata anticipates many ideas of Western poetics such as objective correlative and the holistic approach to aesthetic experience.

Starting with Sri Aurobindo's conceptualisation of poetry as "mantra of the real" R.K. Mishra traces its support in the writings of Plato, Shelley, Abercrombie and others.

Asha Choubey offers a fascinating reading of Sophocles's *Oedipus* in the light of Indian *rasa* theory.

Alka Saxena has discovered an interesting affinity between American fiction of the early twentieth century with the Indo-English fiction of the same period in their concern for the disintegration of values in the wake of wars and political uprisings.

Digambar Singh Dewari shows how Saul Bellow's *Henderson the Rain King* and R.K. Narayan's *The Guide* are marked by a quest motif and mythical underpinnings.

From another angle P.C. Pradhan examines how the quest motif is inscribed in Hermann Hesse's *Siddhartha* which can be seen as Siddhartha's spiritual quest for wisdom and sheds new light on E.M. Forster's *A Passage to India* and Mulk Raj Anand's *Nine Moods of Bharata* in the process.

By writing a novel the novelist writes himself. Ranjit Singh examines some of the novels of Nayantara Sahgal and Akilon, traces the biographical sources of many episodes described in their novels and shows how each recreated her/his life-experience differently in terms of their art.

Sumita Nasker tries to show how Katherine Mansfield's understanding of the ambivalence of life and death finally leads to an integrated outlook in the final scene of *At the Bay,* a story that predates *Mrs. Dalloway* in confining the action to the happenings of one day in the life of a protagonist.

Ameena K. Ansari compares Anjana Appachana's "Her Mother" and Shani Mootoo's "A Garden of Her Own" in terms of the expressions of diaspora and shows how in both the stories the protagonists move from self-pity to self-realisation through self-effacement and reflect in the process, what Atwood calls "Rapunzel" syndrome.

Veena Nare shows, and convincingly, how Santa Rama

Rau's play fails to grasp the magnificence of Forster's novel for lack of artistic vision.

Basavaraj Naikar makes an elaborate comparative study of Graham Greene's *The Power and the Glory* and A. Anantha Murthy's *Samskara* in terms of theme, treatment, narrative strategy and, above all, perceptions of life and religion.

M.A. Nare traces the influence of Buddhist philosophy and the *Jataka* tales in Steinbeck's *The Pearl* and Chaucer's *The Pardoner's Tale* respectively.

Stella looks at the women protagonists of Edith Wharton and Sivasankari and sharply points out their affinities and differences as new women.

Veena Nare picks up Mamta Kalia's poem "Tribute to Papa" and compares it with Sylvia Plath's "Daddy" and argues that Kalia's poem expresses modern sensibility through the use of mask while "Daddy" is a poetic expression of Plath's Electra complex.

Jayanta Bhattacharya in his well-researched paper has examined in detail the expressions of religious thoughts in the poems of Browning and Tagore to underscore the points of affinity between the two poets in their perception of life.

Rama Kundu explores with fine critical insight how Poe's "To Helen" and Jibananda Das's "Banalatā Sen" have a remarkable affinity in theme, mood and poetic texture.

I extend my thanks to the authors for their scholarly contributions to this volume. I shall also like to thank my colleague Professor R. Kundu for assistance in preparing this anthology.

My special thanks go to Dr K.R. Gupta, Managing Director of M/s Atlantic Publishers and Distributors for inviting me to edit this anthology as well as seeing it through the press.

MOHIT K. RAY
Editor

CONTENTS

1

The Western Discovery of Sanskrit and the Growth of Linguistic Studies

AMARNATH JHA

THERE HAS been a hoary tradition of language studies in India dating back to the Vedic times. The *Astadhyayi* of Panini is the culmination of all the previous studies, most of which are now lost. S.K. Belvekar speaks of "nearly a dozen different schools of Sanskrit grammar, at least 300 known from quotations and 'more than a thousand separate treatises, original as well as explanatory'" (1976: 1). "Beside such a concourse, the thousand manuscripts of Priscian's Latin grammar, the pride of our Western tradition," says W.S. Allen, "are but a drop in the grammatical ocean" (1953: 2).

The Indian grammatical systems influenced many nations of the world. The Tamil grammar *Tolkappiyam* (circa 2nd century B.C.), had been influenced by the Sanskrit system. Buddhist monks carried the Indian linguistic scholarship to China. Even the eighth-century Persian grammar by Sibawaih called simply *Al Kitab* is said to be influenced by the Paninian system of classifying the speech sounds from the velum forward (Robins 1967: 98).

The linguistic studies in the West were stimulated by the dissemination of Sanskrit learning during the eighteenth and nineteenth centuries. The Christian missionaries who brought the European languages to India took back with them the Indian linguistic tradition.

Heinrich Roth was a German missionary, who was the first European to compose a Sanskrit grammar. But owing to his untimely death in 1668 at Agra, his work could not be published. The first European grammar of Sanskrit by Paulinus a Sancto Bartholomaeo was written in Latin and published at Rome in 1790. In the field of Sanskrit learning, Germany remained a mediator between India and the rest of Europe and America. Like the fruits of Renaissance and Humanism, the Sanskrit learning spread out westward to stimulate interest in linguistic investigations.

A French missionary, Courdoux, made a comparative study of Sanskrit verbal forms with those in Greek, Latin and other related European languages. But his work could be published only after Sir William Jones'. The most important date serving as a landmark in the spread of Sanskrit learning in the West is that of the year 1786, when Sir William Jones, an English jurist at Calcutta Fort William, addressed the Royal Asiatic Society. The following extract from the speech is perhaps the most quoted of the lines regarding the Indo-European family of languages:

> The Sanskrit language, whatever may be its antiquity, is of a wonderful structure; more perfect than the Greek, more copious than the Latin, and more exquisitely refined than either; yet bearing to both of them a stronger affinity, both in the roots of verbs and in the forms of grammar, than could have been produced by accident; so strong that no philologer could examine the Sanskrit, Greek and Latin, without believing them to have sprung from some common source, which perhaps, no longer exists. There is a similar reason, though not quite so forcible, for supposing that both the Gothic and the Celtic had the same origin with the Sanskrit (Robins 1967: 134).

This observation paved the way for the genealogical classification of languages of which the Indo-European is the leading family. The above pronouncement by Sir William Jones set the Sanskrit ball rolling in the European court. J.R. Firth acknowledges the impact of Sir William Jones' contribution:

> Without the Indian grammarians and phoneticians whom he introduced and recommended to us, it is difficult

> to imagine our nineteenth-century school of phonetics (Allen 1953: 2).

Sir William Jones, however, considered Panini's *sutras* "dark as the darkest oracle" (Ballantyne 1849/1961: ii). "In his 'Dissertation on the Orthography of Asiatic Words in Roman Letters' the whole order of treatment and descriptive technique is clearly based on Indian models" (Allen 1953: 3). He also introduced to the West the Sanskrit classics such as *Shakuntalam, Geetagovindam, Manusmriti* and *Hitopadesha.*

Following Sir William Jones' observation regarding the relationship of Sanskrit with Latin, Greek and Celtic languages, a lot of interest was generated in the study of philology. The nineteenth-century Germany in particular, and Europe in general, witnessed a galaxy of Indologists, interested in every aspect of ancient Indian language, literature and philosophy.

During the nineteenth century a number of textbooks on Sanskrit grammar were written in all the major European languages. Some of them are by Colebrooke, Carey, Wilkins, Forster, Bopp, Monier Williams, Max Muller, H.H. Wilson, Weber, Regnier and Benfey. The books on Sanskrit grammar issued in the latter half of the nineteenth century were more popular than the earlier ones. The first book on Sanskrit grammar to come out in 1879 in the U.S.A. was by W.D. Whitney, who also wrote *Essentials of English Grammar* (1877). MacDowell's *Sanskrit Grammar* was published in 1911. J.R. Ballantyne's translation of *Laghusiddhanta Kaumudi* came out in 1849. Otto Boehtlingk is the first modern European translator of Panini. He collaborated with Rudolf Roth in the gigantic *St. Petersburg Dictionary of Sanskrit.* E.B. Cowell (1826-1903) was the first Professor of Sanskrit at Cambridge. Many of the European universities began courses in Sanskrit. The western interest in Sanskrit learning facilitated the growth of philology. R.H. Robins makes it clear:

> The linguistic study of Sanskrit by Europeans had a twofold effect; the comparison of Sanskrit with the languages of Europe formed the first stage in the

> systematic growth of comparative and historical linguistics, and, additionally, in Sanskrit writings Europeans now came into contact with the independently developed tradition of linguistic scholarship in India, whose merits were acknowledged at once and whose influence on several branches of European linguistics was deep and lasting (1967: 135-36).

Inspired by the Sanskrit learning a few of the Western scholars, who had studied Sanskrit, wrote books on the various aspects of language. The works of Grimm, Verner, Grassmann etc. could not have been so conclusive, had there been no linguistic enlightenment in the wake of Sanskrit studies in the West.

Many of the nineteenth-century philologists were learned in Sanskrit. Max Muller has very correctly stated that "a comparative philologist without a knowledge of Sanskrit is like an astronomer without a knowledge of mathematics" (Crystal 1971: 153). Max Muller himself wrote *Lectures on the Science of Language* (1873), besides his other specialist works on Indological studies. W.D. Whitney, Professor of Sanskrit at Yale during the third quarter of the nineteenth century, wrote several books on language studies, such as *Language and the Study of Language* (1867), *Oriental and Linguistic Studies* (1874) and *The Life and Growth of Language: An Outline of Linguistic Science* (1875).

The historically oriented comparison in the 19th century led to the classification of languages—both genealogical and typological. The Schlegel brothers popularised Sanskrit studies in Germany. A.W. von Schlegel became the first Professor of Sanskrit in the University of Bonn. Adolf von Schlegel initiated the typological classification in 1818. Inflexional languages were supposed to be superior to the analytical languages. The interest in genealogical classification, however, also grew side by side. These studies, as Robins says, "were partly as a result of the stimulus derived from the study of Sanskrit...by Western scholars, and the demonstration at the end of the eighteenth century of the indispensable connection of this language with Latin, Greek and German" (1964: 295).

There had been linguistic studies in the West even before the migration of Sanskrit. Greek language studies dating since the time of Panini passed on through the Romans, the Middle Ages and the Renaissance. Greek grammar by Dionasius Thrax was imitated by the prominent Latin grammarians, Donatus and Priscian. Traditional English grammars have been mostly Latinate for their model. Latinate grammars written by J.C. Nesfield in the first decade of the 20th century "attained almost Biblical authority" (Scott *et al.* 1968/1976: 216).

Language studies continued in Europe upto the eighteenth century before there was any definite impact of Sanskrit studies on them. W.S. Allen is aware of the limitations of the British tradition in the following:

> In phonetics, we all too rarely look back beyond the great names of the nineteenth century—Henry Sweet, A.J. Ellis, Alexander Melville Bell—except occasionally to honour a few lonely and half-forgotten figures of the immediately preceding centuries (1953: 2).

So meagre had been the contributions of the ancient and medieval European phoneticians that W.S. Allen continues:

> Generally speaking the expressions of ancient phonetic thought in the West have little to repay our attention or deserve our respect, whereas Indian sources as ancient or even more ancient are infinitely more rewarding (1953: 2).

"The strong British interest in Phonetics," says R.H. Robins, "can be traced back for some centuries and was reinforced by the Indian tradition" (1964: 378). Henry Sweet, the most prominent of the nineteenth-century linguists, as W.S. Allen writes, "takes over where the Indian treatises leave off—though even in some matters even Sweet could have learnt from them" (1953: 7). In his *A New English Grammar: Logical and Historical* he applies "the latest result of linguistic investigation as far as they bear directly or indirectly on the English language" (1891/1952 Part I: v).

Among the twentieth-century linguists Ferdinand de Saussure, Leonard Bloomfield, J.R. Firth, Roman Jacobson and Rulon Wells refer to some of the ancient Indian linguistic concepts. The concept of "nominal" as opposed to "verbal" style derives from the Sanskrit *sutra* literature. Even Noam Chomsky is aware of the Paninian system of grammar which he regards "as a fragment of such a 'generative grammar,' in essentially the contemporary sense of this term" (1965: v).

There is no gainsaying the fact that linguistics, which is now a very developed discipline of study, had been positively influenced in its early nineteenth-century phase by the advancement of linguistic studies in ancient India.

WORKS CITED

Allen, W.S. *Phonetics in Ancient India* (London: O.U.P., 1953).

Ballantyne, J.R. (trans.). *Laghusiddhanta Kaumudi* (1849; Delhi: Motilal Banarsidass, 1961).

Belvekar, S.K. *Systems of Sanskrit Grammar* (Delhi: Bhartiya Vidaya Bhawan, 1976).

Chomsky, N. *Aspects of the Theory of Syntax* (Cambridge, Mass: MIT Press, 1965).

Crystal, David. *Linguistics* (Harmondsworth: Penguin, 1971).

Robins, R.H. *General Linguistics: An Introductory Survey* (London: Longmans, 1964).

——. *A Short History of Linguistics* (London: Longmans, 1967).

Scott, Bowley, Brockett, Brown and Goddard. *English Grammar: A Linguistic Study of Its Classes and Structures* (1968; London: E.L.B.S. & Heinemann, 1976).

Sweet, Henry. *A New English Grammar: Logical & Historical* Part I (1891; Oxford: Clarendon Press, 1952).

2

East and West: Some Parallels in Indian and Western Poetics

ASHA CHOUBEY

THERE HAS since long been a tendency to point out the dichotomy that exists (?) between Eastern and Western literary concepts. On one hand there have been scholars like Franz Bopp, Grassman, Schiller, Schopenhaur and Nietzsche who have been attracted by the universal appeal of classical Indian thoughts and on the other hand are the detractors who despise all things Indian. However, there may be traced various parallels between Indian and Western literature as well as literary theories. For instance, there has been a spurt in the recent times to trace the affinity between Aristotle's *Poetics* and Indian Dramaturgy. Noted Sanskrit scholar Bharata, while expounding his theory of *Rasa* took into account not only the Indian world-view but also human psychology, which forms the essence of all great literature. His *Rasasutra* has never been refuted though it has been appreciated by several followers of Bharata who have added their own perception to it and have thereby enriched it to a considerable extent. Bharata's *Rasasutra* though conceived in fourth century B.C. holds relevance even today inasmuch as the basic tenets of this principle hold true in the present times as much as they did in the ancient times. This paper seeks to trace some parallels between *anubhava*—a major constituent of *rasa* and T.S. Eliot's concept of objective correlative and also between *sadharanikarana*—another principle implied in *rasa* theory and the concept of negative capability expounded by Keats.

I

In the sixth chapter of *Natyasastra,* Bharata expounds his famous *Rasasutra* as:

> *Vibhavanubhava—vyabhicari-samyogad rasanispattih.*

Which may be translated as this:

> *Rasa* comes from a combination of *vibhavas, anubhavas* and *vyabhicaribhavas* (Masson 1970: 46).

Rasa according to Bharata is poetic pleasure. This pleasure comes only when there is a stimulus or *vibhava* and it does not come to light unless it is manifested through *anubhava.* A dark, deserted place may arouse the emotion of fear hence it will serve as the cause or *vibhava.* This fear in the heart of the character shall not be known unless it is manifested through horripilation and trembling. Thus horripilation and trembling etc. serve as *anubhava.* These manifestations are simply the physical effects of the emotional state (permanent emotion as well as transient emotion). There is and has to be a causal relation between the stimulus and the emotional state experienced and manifested by the character. For instance the dark, lonely place in the above quoted example must inevitably arouse the emotion of fear, hence the manifestation of fear by the character will sufficiently generate the same emotion in the reader. To the contrary if the writer were to present a well-lit, well-inhabited place, and the characters were still to experience fear, the readers shall not be convinced. This disparity between the emotional state shown by the writer and that of the reader will pose serious hindrance in the enjoyment of poetic pleasure or *rasa.* Bharata talks of two types of manifestations—auditory and visual—*angica* and *vacika.* Both these types are essential in a work of literature. Especially in a play the visual manifestation has an important place as it is through this only that the spectator experiences *rasa* or pleasure.

In his essay "Hamlet and His Problems," Eliot puts forward the concept of objective correlative as a kind of mediation between the creator and the reader/spectator. Eliot writes:

> The only way of expressing emotion in the form of art is by finding an 'objective correlative' in other words a set

> of objects, a situation, a chain of events which shall be the formula of the particular emotion, such that when the external facts, which must terminate in sensory experience are given, the emotion is immediately evoked (Eliot 1932: 124-25).

The very word "sensory" denotes physical effect. This effect may be auditory and it may also be visual. Eliot takes into account all stages of emotional process. The principle of "objective correlative" presupposes the existence of an emotion in the heart of the creator prior to its embodiment in the work of literature. The poet/playwright experiences the emotion and then he infuses it into his characters that must manifest it through accurate correlatives so that an exact emotion is produced in the heart of the reader/spectator as well. If at any stage any one element is not proper, the realisation of pleasure suffers. Eliot takes two examples—one to show how objective correlative works for communication and another to show how the writer fails in communicating the emotion in the absence of the same. Lady Macbeth's sleep-walking in Shakespeare's *Macbeth* is taken as a perfect example of "objective correlative." The picture of the lady walking in her sleep, holding a candle brings to the reader's mind her emotional and mental state. The objective correlative here is accurate. The dramatist does not need to say anything. The picture stands as an objective symbol of the emotional state. Shakespeare could not transmit the pleasure of *Hamlet* to reader/spectator as he failed to create an objective correlative for the purpose of communicating Hamlet's agony and dilemma.

Eliot calls *Hamlet* an artistic failure because Hamlet's anguish does not seem accurate in the given situation. Had he been an adolescent, the reader/spectator could still expect—or at least accept, such excessive sentimentality from him but keeping in mind his age and his calibre, one does not understand why he suffers so terribly. Had any other man been in similar situation, he would never undergo the same intensity of anguish. Shakespeare shows such emotional state as is supported neither by the situation nor by the characters. Hence he fails to convince the reader/spectator due to lack of a proper correlative. Thus this principle takes into account the cause as well as the representation of emotional state as manifested through physical effects. Wimsatt and Brooks, however, make a "useful distinction between motive (the reason for an emotion) and objective correlative (the symbol of an emotion)." Quoting Yvor Winters who talks about "motive" as a kind of objective correlative, Wimsatt and Brooks make an illumining suggestion:

> If the poet is to "control" emotion by providing "motives" for it, he is indeed compelled to make use of "a set of objects, a situation, a chain of events." These are objective and can be presented; and since the emotion is generated by these objects and actions and, in so far as it is controlled, is controlled by the selection and rearrangement of these objectified elements, they may fairly be called the "correlative" of the emotion. For whether their "relation" to the emotion is that of cause or of symbolic equivalent, their correlation with the emotion is evident (1957, 1970: 676).

The principle of "objective correlative" has been interpreted variously by various critics. Mattheissen interprets the term to mean a situation or image, which represents the poet's emotion. "Objective correlative" then means the objective, concrete form of the subjective, abstract emotion. Thus "objective correlative" is a means through which the creator can depersonalise even personal emotions while at the same time retaining its human content. The emotional state of fear can be well expressed by trembling and horripilation even without the writer saying a word. While admiring Dante's poetry, Eliot praises his visual imagination or the ability to make the reader see what the poet saw. This is possible only when instead of describing the emotion by the help of words; the writer presents a picture of that emotion which becomes synonymous with the emotion itself. So much so that the very picture evokes the emotion immediately. Ezra Pound's remarks in *The Spirit of Romance* may be noticed:

> Poetry is a sort of inspired mathematics, which gives us equations, not for abstract figures, triangles, spheres

> and the like, but equations for the human emotions (1910: 664).

Objective correlative may be understood as the "equation for the human emotion." Whenever the cause and manifestation are given the emotion shall naturally arise. The picture of Lady Macbeth (on the stage), holding candle and walking in her sleep shall always breed pity in the heart of the reader as it has become the formula for the same. That is to say it is an exact replica of the emotion, a concrete, palpable experience for the abstract emotion, the very image of a particular emotion. While some interpret objective correlative as the effect, some like Fraser understand it as the motive or cause. They feel what Eliot wanted to emphasise is that simply the depiction of emotional state does not convince the reader, it is the responsibility of the writer to show why a character undergoes a particular emotional state.

On close examination one may find a literary equivalent of *anubhava* in T.S. Eliot's principle of "objective correlative." Lady Macbeth walking in her sleep is an example of *angica* or visual correlative whereas Macbeth's speech at the death of his wife is that of *vacika* or auditory correlative. What Eliot takes as the formula of a particular emotion is naturally the inevitable motive and manifestation of the emotional state. If the creator has a proper knowledge of human psychology, he shall necessarily present only such motives and manifestations as are accurate.

Like Eliot, Bharata in his *Rasa* theory presupposes the experience of pleasure in the heart of the creator. The creator then conveys it to the reader/spectator by the help of manifestation or *anubhava*. While depicting the emotion of love the creator is aided by the permanent emotion of love in his own heart. This he projects in his work. The character experiences love which is manifested through various objective presentations. Restlessness, perspiration, trembling and anxiety are some manifestations of love. The reader/spectator experiences the pleasure of *srngara* or love through these external manifestations only. The anguish of Hamlet does not find an objective equivalent hence it fails to transmit the mental agony of Hamlet to the reader/spectator. The reader/spectator may well imagine the anguish of Lady Macbeth, hence her piteous plight is convincing and the speech of Macbeth at her death (Tomorrow, and tomorrow and tomorrow) is also quite comprehensible, as it seems the inevitable consequence of the tragic death of his wife. Lady Macbeth's pitiable condition is caused by her sense of guilt. Hence her guilt is the *vibhava* for *karuna* here. This sufficiently fills Macbeth with grief or *soka.* Since Macbeth's grief is rightly caused by his wife's sad plight, it successfully generates similar emotions in the heart of the reader/spectator. Anyone in Macbeth's place will experience precisely the same emotions. Lady Macbeth's sleep-walking and her repeatedly washing her hands serves as the proper correlative. Hence the poetic pleasure is realised unhindered. It may also be noted that the *vibhava* or cause and *anubhava* or manifestation are inseparable. The *anubhava* or manifestation of the character becomes the cause or *vibhava* of the poetic pleasure for the reader/spectator. The sleep-walking of Lady Macbeth is the manifestation of her anguish but it becomes the cause of grief for Macbeth as well as the reader. It is this that leads to the reader's perfect identification with Macbeth; thereby increasing the scope for poetic pleasure or *rasa.* This is how a perfect syllogism is created which accounts for pleasure or *rasa.* Thus objective correlative is the combination of *vibhava* and *anubhava*—cause and manifestation.

The concept of *anubhava* also takes into account the need for an objective representation of the subjective emotion. The feeling of anguish that is there in the mind of Lady Macbeth cannot be apprehended by the reader/spectator unless it is made objective by her sleep-walking, holding a candle in her hand. Thus the emotion is transmitted through her gesture; to the mind of the reader/spectator thus making the realisation of *karuna Rasa* possible. It generates pity into the mind of the reader. Objective correlative—as various interpretations show—is the cause as well as the effect of an emotional state.

Eliot takes a complete, logical as well as psychological view of emotional states which results in the poetic pleasure. As early as 4th century B.C. Bharata had evinced a similarly holistic approach. One notices that what was conceived by an Indian poetician as early as 4th century B.C. was still considered novel in the 20th century A.D. The principle of *anubhava* or "objective correlative" is relevant even today and it is taken as the best method of poetry. The French symbolists based their theory of symbols on this principle (though they precede Eliot). The *anubhava* or manifestation or "objective correlative" may also be taken as the symbol of emotion. Thus it is that one principle moves through different literary principles in different languages, affirming the essential harmony or oneness of all literatures.

II

For its realisation *rasa* depends on various constituents, but there is one very important aspect which though not explicit, is implied in Bharata's *Natyasastra* and that is the role of the reader/spectator. While defining the mental faculty of *sumana* Bhatta Nayaka calls this state *sadharanikarana* (Gnoli 1985: xv). In the sixth chapter of *Natyasastra,* Bharata writes about *sumanas* by which he seems to mean sensitive reader/spectator, one who has a pure mind. Abhinavagupta in his *Abhinavabharati* has developed this concept of *sumana.* He interprets it in this way:

> ...with a mind that is completely free from any kind of obstructions from any sense organ (*i.e.* completely concentrated) because they are completely absorbed in the thrill of imaginative experience... (Masson 1947: 47).

This freedom from sense organs is a state when the reader goes beyond space and time. This according to Abhinavagupta, is *camatkara.* One must be able to transcend one's ego only then the realisation of *rasa* shall be possible. Bhatta Nayaka calls this state *sadharanikarana*. It is in the context of the reader mainly that the concept of *sadharanikarana* has been expounded. For as long as the reader/spectator remains bound by his ego, he shall not be able to enjoy poetic pleasure. This transcendence leads to generalisation of emotions. *Sadharanikarana* requires total identification of the perceiver with the perceived. This is the ideal state for poetic pleasure. It is a kind of *advaita* or oneness between the perceiver and the object of perception. This is the state when one becomes oblivious of all personal boundaries and goes beyond time and space. This is how pain becomes pleasurable and *karuna* brings joy. Gnoli has summed up Nayaka's reasoning quite beautifully:

> The mysterious conversion of pain into pleasure, which accompanies the full realisation of one's own self, is to be found equally in aesthetic experience, which possesses the magical power of transfiguring the greatest sadness into disinterested pleasure contemplation (1985: xx).

The disinterested pleasure is poetic pleasure which is attained only by shedding all personal considerations. This could be experienced only by attaining freedom from sense organs.

Sadharanikarana is a concept, which has been accepted widely in the sphere of poetry. T.S. Eliot's theory of impersonality bears an affinity to *sadharanikarana.* But the concept that comes greatly close to Abhinavagupta's is the concept of "Negative Capability" as concieved by the poet thinker John Keats. Keats believed that poetic pleasure could not be enjoyed unless self-effacement is practised. This concept was first formulated in December 1817, in his letter of 21 December to George and Tom Keats:

> ...several things dovetailed in my mind, and at once it stuck me, what quality went to form a man of achievement, especially in literature and which Shakespeare possessed so enormously—I mean negative capability—that is when a man is capable of being in uncertainties, mysteries, doubts without any irritable reaching after fact and reason (Forman 1935: 72).

Thus this quality of self-effacement is necessary not only in the perceiver but also in the creator. In order that the reader/spectator may identify with the object, the creator—at the time of creation—must also be able to annihilate his ego. Shakespeare could create Iago as well as Imogen because he could transcend his ego. It is because of this that the reader also enjoys both these characters. Keats compares a poet to a chameleon who changes colour according to the object of his perception. He portrays different objects with equal veracity, which is not possible, if he does not have the ability to depersonalise his personal emotion. Thus, in a way Keats says in the context of the creator what *rasa* theory states in the context of the spectator.

Oscar Wilde in his *The Delay of Lying Intentions* writes:

> The only beautiful things...are the things that do not concern us. As long as a thing is useful or necessary to us, or affects us in any way, either for pain or for pleasure... it is outside the proper sphere of art. To art's subject-matter we should be more or less indifferent (1913: 16-17).

This indifference is an ability to annihilate one's personal identity and to become a part of the universal identity. Unless one achieves this, one cannot enjoy the sublime pleasures afforded by works of art. Personal considerations pose hindrance in the path of aesthetic pleasure. Keats talks about his body becoming numb when he listens to the song of Nightingale ("Ode to Nightingale"); again this numbness of body is tantamount to freedom from sense organs. Shakespeare could create heroes and villains with equal expertise simply because he could set aside or postpone his personal while creating. It is the ability of self-annihilation or generalisation that enables the writer to make his creations enjoyable. Herein one may find another implication that in order that the text may transmit pleasure to the reader, the poet must be able to experience it himself.

Both the principles talk about aesthetic pleasure and both expound the theory of transpersonalisation. Keats stresses the need for negative capability primarily in the creator whereas the Indian masters talk about the spectator. However, in talking about the creator Keats finally comes to the reader/spectator and Bharata starts from the reader and goes on to take the creator's perspective. Thus the concept, like *sadharanikarana* gives as much importance to the poet's feeling as to that of the character and the reader/spectator. Negation of self or ego is tantamount to transpersonalisation—as *sadharanikarana* has been translated by some scholars.

WORKS CITED

Eliot, T.S. *Selected Essays* (1958; London: Faber and Faber, 1932).

Ghosh, Manmohan. *Natyasastra* (Calcutta: Asiatic Society, 1950).

Gnoli, Raniero. *The Aesthetic Experience according to Abhinavagupta* (Varanasi: Chowkhamba Sanskrit Series Office, 1985).

Keats, John. (ed.) Forman, M.B. *Letters* (London: OUP, 1935).

Masson, J.L. and Patwardhan, M.V. *Aesthetic Rapture* vol. 1. (Poona: Deccan College, 1970).

Mattheissen, F.O. *The Achievement of T.S. Eliot* (1947; London: OUP, 1935).

Pound, Ezra. *The Spirit of Romance* (London: OUP, 1910).

Vishveshwar, Acarya (ed. and tr.). *Hindi Abhinavabharati* (Delhi: University of Delhi, 1965).

Wilde, Oscar. *The Delay of Lying Intentions* (London: OUP, 1913).

Wimsatt, William K. and Cleanth Brooks. *Literary Criticism: A Short History* (New Delhi: Oxford and IBH Publishing Co., 1970).

Winters, Yvor. *Anatomy of Nonsense* (Norfolk: New Directions, 1943).

3

Eastern and Western Views on the Poetry of Incantation

R.K. MISHRA

LIKE MOST of the Western poets and critics, Sri Aurobindo an outstanding Indian poet in English enunciated a poetic theory of his own. His concept of poetry evolves from his Yogic experiences as a seer. He conceptualised poetry as the "Mantra of the Real." Such a definition of poetry is inconceivable and unheard of in as much as it has a spiritual implication beyond the conception of modern poets and critics. It sounds implausible and preposterous to them. In order to bring home this concept of Mantric or incantatory poetry in English, Sri Aurobindo relates this phenomenon to Over Head consciousness in terms of which he expounds the origin of this kind of poetry.

In the context of incantatory poetry the sage of Pondicherry defines mantra as the poetic expression of the deepest spiritual reality. "It is the product of overmind." Mantra emanates from the inspiration of this mind. It characterises the language in such a manner that it conveys infinitely something more than mere sense of the words. It is born out of the infinite and dissolves mystically in to the infinite. It is something essentially mystical and spiritual. "Mantra can never be a product of human mind, however brilliant it may be. It is basically concerned with the realisation of some inmost truth of God and self, man and Nature, cosmos and life, thing and thought, and experience and deed."

As regards its mode of expression Sri Aurobindo states that mantric utterance is possible only when three highest intensities of poetic speech meet and become indissolubly one, a highest intensity of rhythmic movement, a highest intensity of verbal form and thought substance of style and a highest intensity of the soul's vision of truth. It is only at a certain height of the fused intensities that mantra is produced. It is the celestial music which is of the utmost spiritual resonance. It is in essence the rhythmic revelation of intuition arising out of the soul's sight of God and Nature. The human soul gets most harmoniously identified with the eternal spirit above.

With regard to the poetry of incantation or mantric poetry Sri Aurobindo points out the distinctive features. This kind of poetry projects the poet's soul that perceives the Divine Truth, the Divine Delight and Divine Beauty. A poet is gifted with an uncommon spiritual insight by virtue of which he perceives the divine beauty and reality hidden from the sight of an ordinary man. He discovers the "intense illumination of speech," those "inspired words and supreme utterances" in which flows the divine rhythmic movement. The spontaneous outburst of these rhythmic movements gives birth to mantric poetry. The true creator and hearer of incantatory poetry is the soul. Poetry becomes incantatory when it is infused with the greater breath of the spirit that elevates earthly life in to a new sublime height of Divinity.

Sri Aurobindo points out the four levels of mind or consciousness from which springs the inspiration for mantric utterances of poetry. They are Higher Mind, Illumined Mind, Intuitive Mind and Over Mind. A poet, who spiritually explores these levels of consciousness, derives divine inspiration, the vital force of creative beauty and the power of transmitting his experiences in the form of mantric poetry. Sri Aurobindo states in his own words, "The voice of poetry comes from a region above us, a plane of our being above and beyond our personal intelligence, a supermind which perceives the innermost and the largest truth and its native language is revelatory, inspired with intuitive words which are vibrant or densely packed with glory of ecstasy and lustre."

Sri Aurobindo's interpretation of incantatory poetry is highly metaphysical and hence it is esoteric. In this context, the views of the Western mind throw some light on the theory of mantric poetry. The Western critics contend that the highest reach of poetry is attainable only when the words and ideas are transformed through some mysterious power into a form of incantation and thereby acquire an irresistible haunting power over the hearer's or reader's mind. In this context, Plato's view is worth mentioning. Plato spoke of how poets were possessed by the muses and how they composed poems as though they were inspired by some frenzy. In fact, he was referring to such art of incantation into which poetry dissolved itself. Plato in his "Phaedrus" and "Ion" where the poet is presented as the inspired rhapsodist first stated this concept of poetry. It is through the tone of the inspired poet that God Himself speaks. Socrates speaks to Ion, "The gift, which you possess is not an art but an inspiration: there is a divinity moving you." All good poets of epics as well as lyrics compose their beautiful poems not by art but because they are inspired and possessed. Although the word incantation is not used here yet we may assume it to be implied by Plato. David Daiches, a great critic of poetry too accepts this Platonic concept of poets and poetry. He comments, "the poet was a possessed creature not using language in the way that normal human beings do but speaking in a divinely inspired frenzy." This is illustrative of how the Western view of poetry stated in the earliest period of human civilisation gains acceptance in the modern age.

Another poet, who believed in the power of incantatory poetry, was the romantic poet Shelley. He invokes the West Wind to disseminate his revolutionary ideas all over the universe by the incantation of his poetry. He writes in the concluding stanza of the "Ode to the West Wind":

> And by the incantation of this verse Scatter, as from an unextinghished hearth Ashes and sparks spread among mankind.

Among the modern critics, who are preoccupied with this theory of incantatory poetry are Abercrombie and C.D. Lewis. They discuss the incantatory power and effects of English poetry. According to Abercrombie "the first thing that we require of all poetry is incantation, the power of using words so as to produce in us a sort of enchantment." This power of incantation is not at all a matter of technique or craftsmanship and yet it is through the quality of words that the critical mind will be able to lay hold on the power of incantation which is the hallmark of all true and great poetry.

To Abercrombie, the poet's real creative power lies in the ability to explore and acquire those magical words and phrases by force of which he is able to communicate the vibrant experiences of his mind. The poet's power of incantation lies in creating a unique, individual vibrant psychological state in the reader or listener by the power of words and phrases.

Similarly C.D. Lewis too supports this view of incantatory or mantric poetry. He holds the view that "Poetry has its roots in incantation" and that its effect has always been to create a state of mind that can realise the Beauty, Delight and Truth. He stated that poetry is born out of magic, it grew up with religion. Lewis does not deal much elaborately with this subject of mantric poetry but he believes firmly in the spiritual significance of this kind of poetry.

Among the Western critics, James Cousins deals with the concept of mantric poetry in his book *New Ways in English Literature*. He states in the identical manner that mantric poetry elevates the mind of the poet to the level of integral truth that manifests through the incantatory lines that flow spontaneously out of a divinised mind. The fundamental motive of mantric poetry, according to Cousins, is to reach out and lay hold on "something stable behind the instability of word and deed."

As we discuss Sri Aurobindo's views on mantric poetry we find that in his large spiritual utterance, the whole incantation particularly as explained by Western critics like David Daiches, Abercrombie, C.D. Lewis and James Cousins tends to gain some mystical power that manifests from mantric utterances. Sri Aurobindo interprets mantric poetry as the highest intense revealing form of poetic thought and expression. The seer poet explains his theory of poetry neither in the light of ancient Vedic concept nor Western views of incantatory poetry. His interpretation is based upon his own spiritual experiences of mantric poetry that originates in a higher level of Over Head consciousness. Clear cut definition of mantric poetry has been given by Sri Aurobindo in the extract of a verse illustrated below:

> As when the mantra sinks in Yoga's ear its message enters stirring the blind brain
> And keeps in the dim ignorant cell
> its sound:
>
> ....
>
> He meets the deeper listening of his soul:
> The word repeats itself in rhythmic strains:
>
> ....
>
> All knowledge rushes on him like a sea
> Transmutated by the white spiritual ray
> He walks in naked heavens of joy and calm
> Sees the god-face and hears transcendent speech.

This particular extract authenticates Sri Aurobindo's views of poetry as mantra. No classical literary critic had ever defined poetry as incantation. He points out that his long epic "Savitri" is mantric in sound and effect. He attributes its versification to divine inspiration and not to his own creation. It was written in a state of Yogic realisation. In this epic, we hear the vibration of a new kind of rhythm which is incantatory. In the context of the mantric effects of "Savitri," K.D. Sethna quotes many lines from the epic to establish his views about the flow of incantatory force through the lines: "Sight sound waves are breaking from the soul's great deeps." This is a striking example of mantric utterance.

Since Sri Aurobindo's theory is supported by the ancient Vedic and Upanishadic concept of poetry, it stands incontrovertible among the Indian critics. No Eastern critic, who believes in spiritual and Yogic experiences can deny the views. Sri Aurobindo's views are strengthened and are supported by the Western critics like Plato, Shelley, David Daiches, Abercrombie, C.D. Lewis and James Cousins.

WORKS CITED

Cousins, H. James. *Aurobindo Ghose the Philosopher as Poet*: *New Ways in English Literature* (Madras: Sterling, 1972).

Ghose, Sri Aurobindo. *The Future Poetry* (Pondicherry: Sri Aurobindo Ashram, 1953).

Gokak, V.K. *Sri Aurobindo and Aesthetics.* Mother India, January, 1954.

Iyengar, K.R.S. *Indian Writing in English* (New Delhi: Sterling, 1985).

——, (ed.). *Sri Aurobindo* (Calcutta: Arya Publishing House, 1950).

Langley, G.H. *Sri Aurobindo: Indian Poet Philosopher and Mystic* (London: David Marlow, 1949).

Nanda Kumar, Prema. *Sri Aurobindo: A Critical Introduction* (Pondicherry: Sri Aurobindo Ashram, 1962).

——. *A Study of Savitri* (Pondicherry: Sri Aurobindo Ashram, 1976).

Ramaswami, S. and Seetaramaya, V.S. *English Critical Tradition* (Pondicherry: Sri Aurobindo Ashram, 1982).

4

Sophocles and Indian Poetics: A Study of *Oedipus* in the Light of *Rasa* Theory*

ASHA CHOUBEY

THE AIM of literary theory is and should be to enhance the pleasure afforded by a literary genre, but not all theories prove true in this respect. While some border simply on mental exercise, some believe more in shredding the work of literature to pieces than in increasing the reader's enjoyment. Such theories meet their end as soon as they rise, because though they may have some strong philosophical implications, they are not practicable. There are but some theories which stand the test of time and continue to hold their currency and relevance even after some centuries. *Rasa* theory propounded by Bharata in his *Natyasastra* is one such theory which has helped derive pleasure out of many great works of literature. If it is applied judiciously, it can bring out the subtleties and complexities of a work of art and thus enhance our sense of pleasure. Its great practicability and its emphasis on "pleasure" account for its popularity wide and large. As a theory focusing chiefly on aesthetic relish or pleasure, *rasa* theory can be successfully applied to literature of various languages. Just as the *rasa* theory is the fruit of the critical genius of a great Indian master, *Oedipus* is the progeny of the literary genius of an equally great Greek master.

* The paper was presented at the International Seminar on 'The Relevance of Ancient Classics in the New Millennium' organised by The Heritage Trust and Department of Ancient History and Culture, M.J.P. Rohilkhand University on 4-8 February 2000.

Moreover, India and Greece may boast of being the inheritors of two of the most ancient and rich cultures. Hence, what can be more interesting than making an attempt to relish the fruit of the Greek master's labour in the light of the Indian aesthetics—*rasa* theory? Such comparative study shall enable us to have a clear cut idea of Western and Eastern aesthetics, and a comparative analysis of Eastern concepts of literary theories applied on Greek drama will not only enhance our knowledge of the art of drama but also sharpen our intellectual insight and add new dimensions to the existing scholarship. This paper may be seen as a humble attempt in this direction.

I

Rasa theory propounds a principle which is quite significant in its own right. *Rasa* is a word which may lead to confusion as it is a broad-spectrum word which has different meanings in different contexts. In the *Natyasastra* Bharata expounds the famous *Rasasutra* as:

> *Vibhavanubhava-vyabhicari-sanyogad rasanispatih*

Which may be translated like this:

> The realisation of *rasa* results from the union of three elements—*vibhava*, *anubhava* and *vyabhicari*.

Since *rasa* is realised by the union of its constituents, it may be taken as a process. In this process the permanent emotions are indispensable as it is they that result in *rasa*. These permanent emotions are also the principle emotions in the processing of *rasa*. The permanent emotion, however, is not perceptible through the senses. It has to be manifested through *anubhavas*. *Rati* or love is a permanent emotion but it resides in the heart and is not known unless manifested through restlessness, inconstancy, anxiety, trembling and other such symptoms. Again, though a person in love may experience these various emotional states he/she shall be undergoing the experience of love only as these are all related to the principal emotion of love. In this sense anxiety as subsidiary to love is different from anxiety as subsidiary to fear because though the emotional state of anxiety is one, the root or the permanent emotion is altogether different. The subsidiary or the subordinate emotional state is what Bharata calls *vyabhicari bhavas. Vyabhicari* denotes a movement or a fleeting state. Thus, through a permanent emotion a subject may experience several transient states, but basically he shall then be undergoing the experience of the principal emotion only. Once we have translated the *bhavas* as states, the confusion clears to a great extent. Priyadarshi Patnaik translates the permanent emotion as stable state and transient emotion as transitory state (Patnaik 1997: 29). Bharata also mentions *vibhava* and *anubhava* hence we need to understand them. In order that an emotion may be aroused, there has to be some cause or stimulus. Given a cause an emotion is aroused but it cannot be known unless it is manifested. Hence, while considering a particular emotion, we need to take into account its cause and manifestations.

One may notice that *rasa* theory takes a logical, psychological and scientific view of the aesthetic pleasure. It examines and embraces in its fold all possible aspects of poetic enjoyment. The cause, the transitory state, the outward manifestation (both auditory and visual) and the final experience come in its purview. It lays emphasis on the role of the spectator or audience for generalisation. This concept implies the universality of the object of contemplation. The aesthetic pleasure can be had only when one's mind is free of individual biases. This state is known as *sadharanikaran.* Abhinavagupta calls this state of mind *camatkara,* when the reader or audience is immersed in the wonderful bliss provided by poetry. Until and unless the reader identifies with the emotion in the text his enjoyment cannot be complete. Abhinavagupta further elaborates the idea by suggesting that *rasa* is *alaukica* which may be translated as ethereal or celestial. He explains by telling us that when we enter the theatre, we go beyond the boundaries of space and time. He compares this literary experience to a wondrous flower which has no beginning and will not end.

II

Before striving to apply *rasa* theory on *Oedipus* plays, we would do better to take a perspective of Sophoclean art. Since Aristotle took *Oedipus* as a model, one may wrongly believe that tragedy, as defined by him, represents the vision of Sophocles. This will be an assumption taken in haste. Aristotle believes that tragedy is an imitation (mimesis) of an action which goes to show that action is the most important element in a play and character deserves a back seat. Even Greek political thought regarded the state as superior to individual. But then, there was also a recognition that state could be best served by individuals who have distinguished themselves by their excellence. Excellence could be achieved by men who are strong individuals. In fact, the whole concept of tragedy becomes absurd if the tragic protagonist is not taken as an individual in his own right. The element of choice is quite important. The tragic hero must not be under compulsion so that given a certain situation he acts in a certain manner which causes doom. The reader must be allowed—rather encouraged and compelled to feel that if the character had not acted in a specific manner, he would be safe. The element of necessity is antithetical to the concept of tragedy. Periclean Athens recognised men as individuals like Elizabethan England. McCollom writes: "The plays of Sophocles...are the greatest surviving monument to Greek individualism" (1994: 159). The Sophoclean hero is one who is fully answerable and responsible for his action as he thinks and acts for himself.

Rasa being pleasure must be closely related to—rather dependent on the world-view of the people. What gives pleasure to the people depends on what their philosophy of life is? People from one culture may enjoy a particular emotion which may not be as enjoyable to those from other cultures. While talking about Indian context one has to note that selflessness is beauty (Kapoor 1998: 97). It is this selflessness of heart that results in compassion and *karuna*. Compassion brings calm of mind—"at peace with oneself" (*Ibidem*). This calm of mind is tranquility or *santa* as acknowledged by Abhinavagupta. Thus compassion and tranquility emerge as the two emotions which are of crucial importance, as far as Indian psyche is concerned. The Western concept after Aristotle takes into account pity and fear as two basic emotions for a work of literature.

A characteristic phrase in Aristotle's discussion of tragedy (and of epic for in this respect he declines to distinguish between the two genres) is "the appropriate kind of pleasure." The appropriate kind being in this case that which accompanies the emotions of pity and fear. To afford this pleasure is in Aristotle's view the function of tragedy, its purpose and end. In this definition of the purpose of tragedy, we can now recognise a further manifestation of the entirely traditional assumption that tragedy exists to give pleasure, and specifically the pleasure of emotional response to its audiences. To be sure, Aristotle is aware that the gratification of the audience's taste can corrupt the tragic art; but this does not lead him to abandon the principle.

That *Oedipus* is taken as a model by Aristotle is common knowledge, now it needs to be seen how far the beauty of *Oedipus* can be enjoyed by the help of Indian aesthetics which is based on *karuna* and *santa*. *Oedipus* is a tragedy of parricide, incest, suicide and self-mutilation. In India, drama was supposed to create aesthetic sentiment and anything which could not do so was avoided. Indian philosophy believes in happy world order and in peace. Hence as a rule Sanskrit drama does not end in tragedy. In fact, Sanskrit plays ended with benediction. Except Bhasa's *Urubhanga*, we don't have a tragedy in Sanskrit literature. *Oedipus* being a tragedy, merits appreciation in the light of *karuna rasa*. The features of *karuna* or the compassionate as analysed by Bharata are as follows:

> Now (the *rasa*) known as *karuna* arises from the permanent emotion of sorrow. It proceeds from *vibhavas* such as curse, affliction (*klesa* of affliction of curse), separation from those who are dear, (their) downfall, loss of wealth, death and imprisonment or from contact with misfortune (*vyasana*), destruction (*upaghata*) and calamity (*vidrava*) (*Aesthetic Rapture* Vol. 1: 52).

A keen examination will show that all these external manifestations are common to both *raudra* and *karuna*. For example, curse is the cause for *karuna* but it is at the same time the external manifestation for *raudra*, similarly death and destruction are also results of *raudra*. Hence these two *rasas* are entwined to some extent in a tragedy.

III

Oedipus Rex opens in an atmosphere of gloom, with the citizens of Thebes showing "all the signs of sickness which is ravaging the city" and "adopting attitudes of desperation and prayer" (7). These descriptions set the tone for pity as well as *karuna*. The opening speech of *Oedipus* illumines the pathos of the atmosphere:

> In the city I hear prayers for the sick.
> And the sound of weeping. The air is heavy.
> With incense and tears (7).

This description again moves the heart of the reader/spectator with pity, hence, if Aristotle's catharsis is at play here, Bharata's *karuna* is not far away. Up to this juncture we find depression and despondency in the atmosphere. However, this despondency soon gives way to resolve or *mati* when we find Oedipus assuring the citizens with the words:

> I can't rely on second hand reports,
> I have come to find out for myself.
> I am Oedipus the king. Everyone knows my name (7).

These words show Oedipus' confidence in his abilities, hence the apparent transient emotion is that of resolve. If it is resolve, even resolve cannot be taken as the transient emotion for *karuna* so the reader may be confused for a while. However, when we take into account the fact that Oedipus is a story well-known to all and as such the reader/spectator knows beforehand that no matter howsoever brave and intelligent the king, he will not be able to improve matters as he shall be rendered helpless. This knowledge serves to increase the grief or *soka*. Soon we find that resolve is replaced by *trasa* or alarm and *cinta* or painful reflection in the priest's description of the chaotic state prevailing in the city:

> This city is like a warship, defeated in battle
> Wallowing aimlessly in a sea blood
> The crops are rotting in the fields
> Disease is killing all the cattle,
> Babies are born dead, or decay in the womb,
> And as if that were not enough, some god has sent plague,
> Like a fire-demon to scorch our people (8).

This presents a picture of despair as rotting of crops and dying of babies signify end of all life. Life is being crushed even as it originates hence future seems to be bleak. The city has been reduced into a cemetery where no sign of life is to be seen since God-sent plague is a suggestion of the calamity which is perhaps beyond human power. All this serves to heighten the pathos which reaches zenith in the realisation that the hapless Thebans have placed all their hopes for redemption in the able leadership of Oedipus who is himself doomed. The sense of pity that moves the reader's heart is aggravated at intervals by Oedipus' continued assurance and self-confidence:

> Whatever the oracle demands you have word
> Will be meticulously performed (9).

Had the reader not known Oedipus' story, he would find some relief in these intervals but since Oedipus is common knowledge, here even resolve does not provide any relief. Creon has been sent by Oedipus to find out the cause of misery and at the sight of him returning, Oedipus derives consolation:

> Whatever the message, he is certainly smiling
> Apollo god of healing let the news be good (9).

But the reader continues to float on despondency and despair the cause of which seems to be *moha* or delusion of Oedipus. When Oedipus is informed of the root cause of this calamity he is agitated and also impatient to find out the culprit. Though agitation may be taken as transient emotion for the compassionate; impatience, and curiosity to know is not so. But it serves to add to the grief of the reader as this impatience to know someone outside of himself turns out to be his self-realisation.

Oedipus stands as a dispenser of justice but at the end of it all he shall find himself at the receiving end. When at the height of agitation he says: "Justice for Laius/ And my own safety go hand in hand" (11), he does not know the implications of what he says. But the reader who is omniscient in Oedipus' case is moved to tears at the anticipation of waste of so much benevolence. Since Oedipus is sure that he shall resolve the crisis soon, the counsellors are also hopeful.

Oedipus being a charitable, amicable king does not pronounce capital punishment even on a stranger. When such a man meets his doom not only the emotion of pity and fear aggravate but also the effect of compassionate increases.

The beauty of *Oedipus* comes to a great extent from the juxtaposition of two paradoxical attitudes or points of view or emotions. As in the messages of Creon and the Corinthian. On entering Creon conveys a paradoxical message:

> It will be good news if all turns well
> Though perhaps painful to begin with (10).

This message of Creon may be compared with that of the Corinthian:

> I come from Corinth, and my message
> Is bound to please you; though it's painful too,
> And will make you sad to begin with (39).

These two messages are similar not only in their content, and phrases but also in the fruit that they bring. We may say that Creon and the Corinthian are two harbingers of disaster in the play and both come with identical messages. This message is again one of grief as well as happiness and it is the intermingling of both that the *rasa* is produced. After all isn't life a combination of joy and sorrow? And also isn't it because of this play of light and shadow that we love it so much? In Oedipus' dialogue with Teiresias, Sophocles juxtaposes two seemingly opposite attitudes. While Oedipus is in a flurry and quite furious, the attitude of Teiresias is one of constraint and extreme self-control: "Lose your temper, shout, stamp if that pleases you. I shall say nothing more" (19).

Again the beauty of emotions increases here only because of the fore knowledge on the part of the reader of the futility of Oedipus' pride. Hence, the enjoyment or relish of *rasa* increases only for those who know what is going to happen next, while for those who have absolutely no knowledge of and no acquaintance with Oedipus, the enjoyment lies not so much in compassion as in modulation of their curiosity and resultant suspicion.

One may note some beautiful, exciting parallels between Indian and Greek aesthetics. Aristotle while examining *Oedipus*, pointed out two elements out of which the tragedy progresses peripeteia and anagnorisis. These two also serve as the cause of *karuna* in the case of Oedipus. Oedipus, when we meet him for the first time, is a strong and well trusted king. His people have complete confidence in him, not only because he is a brave and benevolent man, but also because he has miraculous powers. He has in the past saved the country from the Sphinx. He is on the whole at the height of his glory but for him reversal of fortune comes very early in the shape of the curse to his country. The curse which has come upon his people is the doing of a supernatural power or God and in order to resolve the crisis he takes the help of God himself. This self-discovery or self-realisation on the part of Oedipus is anagnorisis or recognition. Self-discovery of Oedipus again generates the transient emotion of the *vibodha* or awakening. This recognition leads to much grief and in this sense it may be seen as the cause of *karuna*. In *Oedipus Rex,* it comes out of Teiresias' parting shot: "...To this children/ Whom he loves, he is brother and father:/ To the woman who bore him lover and son./ To his father, a killer and the man who supplants him" (23).

The revelation and prophecy of Teiresias leaves the Thebans in turmoil. They are in a state of confusion, fright and panic. They are as if in apprehension and sometimes even in stupor:

> I'm like jelly, uncertain
> What's happening or will happen (24).

Most of the emotions and emotional states in *Oedipus* plays are overlapping and interchanged and the play is lovelier because of this. Creon has been a loyal friend and relative but Oedipus doubts his integrity and openly accuses him of plotting to overthrow his rule. Creon is, naturally, hurt and does not hide his indignation. Indignation is the transient emotion of *karuna*. It must melt the heart of the reader with compassion for Creon, instead the reader sympathises with Oedipus because he knows that Creon's indignation is the precedent of his hatred for Oedipus, and now the already hapless Oedipus has added to his miseries by doubting and making foe out of a friend.

Irony, especially tragic irony plays an important role in a tragedy. In Bharata the tragic irony is delusion of mind or *bhrama*. Jocasta herself becomes the victim of ignorance: "That's how much oracles are worth. In future/ Whatever they say one way or the other I won't waste my time with any of them!" (37). On entering the palace, the Corinthian first meets Jocasta and blesses her with words which acquire special, deeper significance though they are said in a innocent manner. He says: "God bless her then and all her family/ Bearing children to such a great man" (39). We know, in fact, the tragedy takes place because Jocasta is the wife of Oedipus and has given birth to his children.

A tragic hero is a serious, sober man and so is Oedipus, but at times he loses self-control. The Corinthian breaks the sad news of his father's death to the king and the reader naturally expects lamentations from him instead he bursts with joy: "Well then Ha! What now Jocasta I was the man./ Who would kill my father... and so is the oracle and his prophecies,/ Dead and rotten" (40). Here the dementedness of Oedipus is the *anubhava* or manifestation of joy or *hasya* but becomes the *vibhava* for *karuna* in the heart of the reader. From this point the pathetic situation becomes even worse as every piece of information given by the Corinthian to relieve Oedipus turns out to be another nail in the latter's coffin.

As far as the consummation of *rasa* is concerned according to the Indian standards the compassionate must culminate in *santa* or tranquil. In *Oedipus at Colonus* one comes across variegated aspects of the same. The scene is set in front of a grove sacred to the furies. This setting gives rise to a number of transient emotions. There is apprehension, gloom, despair, melancholy and despondency. Then Oedipus enters, blind and dressed in rags making the picture even bleaker. This presents a brilliant example of *dainya* or depression. Oedipus strikes as a poor soul at the mercy of his daughters. Gone is the confidence, the powerful thundering voice and the commanding personality. However there is less of lamentation and agitation as now he seems to have reconciled to fate. Depression has given way to hope and when the local man informs him that the place is sacred to furies. The transient emotion that can be experienced is of resolve and assurance. Though his plight now is worse than what it was at the end of *Oedipus Rex*, he seems to have acquired *dhrti* or contentment and despondency, dejection, and desperation are gone. It's a kind of awakening and resolve that he has acquired:

> And now I feel certain great goddesses,
> Daughters of darkness and the night's terrors.
> That you have guided me to your sacred place (71).

Assurance, and contentment are not ordinarily the transient emotions of *karuna* but this is no ordinary situation. Not for a moment does the reader forget that this is Oedipus the powerful, intelligent and revered king of Thebes who has been reduced to a shadow. Hence contentment on his part may be transient emotion but for the reader it becomes the cause of *karuna*.

A crucial issue needs consideration here as to what exactly is a perfect tragedy? *Oedipus Rex* where the atmosphere of gloom is so impenetrable and complete that it does not end in *santa*? Or *Oedipus at Colonus* where the atmosphere is so steeped in *santa*, that even the intermittent specks of pathos fail to picture misery as they are supposed to do? Whether one applies Aristotle's *Poetics* or the Indian *Natyasastra*, one has to agree that the tranquil must be the end of tragedy. According to Aristotle, tragedy must lead to *catharsis* or purgation of soul. This is a stage when mind is relieved of all tensions and passions subside. "Calm of mind, all passions spent" and in India the *santa rasa* denotes similar state. Though this seems a later addition. Abhinavagupta quotes Bharata: People devoid of passion (take delight) in *moksa* (N.S. XVII, 58, *santa rasa:* 137).

However the permanent emotion related to *santa* is *nirveda* or indifference or renunciation and *sama* which may be translated as calmness. The end of tragedy then, must be marked by *santa*. *Oedipus Rex* ends with Creon providing shelter to Oedipus and promising to take good care of his daughters. Chorus follows with the message:

> Judge no man's life until he is dead
> There are no wonders till the race is run.
> Call no man fortunate, or safe from pain.
> Till he lies in his last ever-lasting bed
> And the earth covers his head (61).

As far as world-weariness and feeling of renunciation are concerned, the message seems to suggest some, but it still does not culminate into *santa*. *Oedipus at Colonus* is strewn with passages denoting the permanent emotion of indifference right from the beginning. In fact, Oedipus' reconciliation with loss and consecutive recovery is a kind of *nirveda* only. Chorus depicts the mood of Oedipus and sets the tone for *santa*:

> Later or sooner the same death
> Not with marriage songs. But funeral weeping
> Delivers us all to earth (107).

The chorus seems to be preparing for the finale when it says:

> ...Youth soon passes
> Like a carnival of frivolity: horror, war and carnage,
> Old age only increase
> The torment, short of friend and breath, you stagger on
> Towards the last crisis (108).

Polynices attempts to take his father back to get him to intervene between the two brothers, but he is refused and also cursed by Oedipus. When he leaves, the chorus again philosophies about man's fate, therein manifesting the permanent emotion of indifference:

Time is the eye of mortality
Watching some men rise, and some go under
On the wheel of destiny (115).

The death of Oedipus takes place in an atmosphere steeped in the tranquil. The reader gets to experience the marvellous (*adbhuta*), the compassionate (*karuna*) and the *santa* alternately. The time, symptom and the manner of Oedipus' death had been prophesied by the gods. When the thunder sounds Oedipus knows that death is close at hand. Here the permanent emotion of surprise comes to the fore:

And now the lightening!
Could the message be any plainer
The thunder god speaks and brandishes his brightening
Firebrands! Gods only appear
Like thus when something tremendous is happening (110).

Here we get to see Sophoclean philosophy of death which is kindred to that of Indian thinkers. Death is not the end of life, it is simply a new beginning, hence there is no cause for despair. The death of Oedipus takes place in strange, mysterious manner. Where the sustaining emotion is *adbhuta*:

The angle of death is here Hermes
Himself I feel his chilly finger (119).

From the time Oedipus walks towards his death, the chorus takes a contemplative turn and philosophies on the mystery of this world. It prays for justice and peace to Oedipus:

Let him take his place on the dark plain
Walking the endless fields of night
Unjust persecution, pain
And suffering were his destiny
Justice at the end is his right (119).

Chorus, in fact, prepares ground for the *santa*, that is underlying the theme when it says, "Let him pass in peace and quietness" or "muzzle the beast and bless/ His passing with eternal sleep" (120). The reader experiences the rise and fall of indifference all through. Even his death does not evoke pity so much as indifference because death is the end of all his sorrows. His death, in this sense is full of hope for him. He has to be an instrument in the hands of gods, and also his death will bring blessing for Athenians.

The daughters of Oedipus—Antigone and Ismene are the only souls who are aggrieved. But this pall of gloom is dispelled when Theseus consoles them and tells them that their lamentations must come to an end, and they must try to accept the design of God: "Over Indulgence in grief, when miraculous favours have been granted, will make them angry" (126). This assurance serves to dispel all *sanka* or apprehension and brings about *dhrti* or contentment. The final chorus presents the transient emotion of renunciation again thereby establishing the supremacy of *santa* or tranquility:

> Now sorrow has run its full course
> And tears must end
> These events have come to a just close
> On holy ground
> The gods are eternal and the life of man
> A speck of dust on a great plain (127).

Tragedy is valuational. The quest of the protagonist is always a search for good life. It is in this quest that he evolves as a human being. Oedipus in *Oedipus Rex* may be a social outcast but towards the end he becomes a better and wiser man. The pain that the tragic hero suffers is his ordeal by fire out of which he emerges stronger and holier. McCollom writes: "The Sophoclean hero thinks and acts for himself and his independence isolates him" (162). However, Oedipus' search for identity leads not only towards self-discovery but the discovery of general good as well. T.R. Henn while defining tragedy writes: "Of it's (tragedy's) fruits the greatest is self-knowledge through suffering" (1961: 292). This is what happens in *Oedipus*. The self-realisation of Oedipus does not remain personal, it becomes cosmic and this cosmic view brings Sophocles closer to Indian aesthetics. Near the end Oedipus becomes a saintly figure who has no prayer for himself. Instead he prays for the world.

Aristotelian tragic heroes gain our sympathy, but looking at their stories we can confidently say that if such and such had not committed this or that mistake he would not have suffered. Though the character is not villainous, one can put the blame on him. But about Oedipus one does not know how one could change his story. Even if Oedipus had not been a person of mercurial temperament, he would still suffer as much as he did. In the case of Aristotelian tragic hero character is destiny, but in the case of Oedipus destiny becomes the omnipotent force. This may also account for the *karuna*. We pity Othello, we pity Hamlet but no other hero moves our heart as much as Oedipus. Hence in none of the above mentioned tragedies do we experience so much of *karuna* as in *Oedipus* plays. Absence of hamartia may safely be taken as a cause for *karuna* in these plays. H.D.F. Kitto feels that if Oedipus had not come out of Corinth in his self-confidence that he would prove the God wrong, he would never meet his doom. He says that Apollo simply prophesied, he did not compel. Hence Oedipus shall not be fully absolved. A tragedy presupposes the freedom of individual. Unless the tragic hero be a conscious agent, tragedy is not possible.

The strong individuality of a Sophoclean hero may be seen in the almost pagan like defiance of the eternal design. Oedipus, even when he has become a pauper, does not submit before gods. Gods make him an instrument for the welfare of Athens but they have to accept him as he is. He keeps throwing the gauntlet before them. He challenges them and it is in this fortitude that the essence of Sophoclean tragedy lie. Don Taylor writes: "Genuine tragedy in this sense is an essentially pagan idea. Christians must eventually submit, but Greek tragic heroes never do" (1986: XLII). In Sophocles, God is a remote and unappeasable force. If his heroes have an antagonist, it is God. The human value of his plays rises when we find that in the battle for supremacy, it is the man who wins; Oedipus does not cringe before gods. Gods cannot operate without him and are dependent on him in order to make their presence felt. They need him in order to bring blessings to Athens. This unparalleled image of man makes Sophocles the great dramatist that he is.

WORKS CITED

Henn, T.R. *The Harvest of Tragedy* (London: Metheun, 1961).

Kapoor, Kapil. *Literary Theory* (New Delhi: Affiliated East-West Press Pvt. Ltd., 1998).

Kitto, H.D.F. *Greek Tragedy* (London: Metheun, 1950).

Masson, J.L. and Patwardhan, M.V. *Aesthetic Rapture*, Vol. 2, (Poona: Deccan College).

Patnaik, Priyadarshi. *Rasa in Aesthetics* (New Delhi: D.K. Printworld Pvt. Ltd., 1997).

Taylor, Don. *The Theban Plays* (London: Metheun, 1986). (All textual references to Oedipus plays are from this edition.)

McCollom, William G. *Tragedy* (New York: MacMillan & Co., 1957).

5

A Comparative Study of American and Indo-English Fiction in the Early Twentieth Century

ALKA SAXENA

FOR ACADEMICIANS and particularly the admirers of Ernest Hemingway, 21st July 1999 had a special significance. The day marked the hundredth birth anniversary of one of the foremost novelists of the twentieth century. Hemingway enjoyed immense fame and fortune during his lifetime. He started his literary career in a strife-torn world. He was driven by the warring world and learnt to survive by himself. He was the spokesman of the lost generation. His literary style is universally recognised as one of the important innovations of the twentieth century. He brought vigour and fresh life to the American novel.

The twenties was the Hemingway decade, though he did not get the Nobel Prize until 1954. It was in the year 1954 that Hemingway was involved in two major air crashes within two days. According to his wife Mary, both his scalp and skull were laid open and cerebral fluid oozed out. During these accident prone days of January 1954 Hemingway read many obituaries of himself while resting in bed. Miraculously, Hemingway survived and it was in July 1961, that his admirers all over the world were shocked to hear the news of his death. On 2nd July, 1961, when his body betrayed him, Hemingway loaded his double barrel Boss shot gun and pressed it against his forehead and tipped the hammers of the gun. Once more obituaries appeared on the front pages, everywhere. When Hemingway had first read his own obituaries in Nairobi he was amused but now he was past amusement.

The literary scene in America in the early twentieth century was bleak. In the early decades of the twentieth century America was itself a wasteland. Many writers had left the country for the more stimulating atmosphere of post-war Europe. In the period between the two World Wars, literature in the United States scaled a new height of technical perfection. In these years the first important experimental works of Ernest Hemingway and his contemporaries like Scott Fitzgerald, Dos Passos and Cummings, were published and immensely appreciated. The writers of this period found themselves in a world largely dominated by the code of war.

The study of Indo-English writings of the early twentieth century reveals that this period was one of the most turbulent in Indian history. There was a decadence in the Indian ethos. Indo-English literature of the twenties reflects a chaotic scenario. The perennial struggle of the individual against social compulsions is a continuing cause of violence and appears as a theme in Indo-English Fiction. The revolutionary movements of the twentieth century are distinctly visible in the fiction of this period. A comparative study of American and Indo-English literature of the early twentieth century is a challenging and rewarding endeavour.

Rabindra Nath Tagore played a crucial role in both reflecting and moulding the intellectual, social and cultural climate, specially in resurgent Bengal. Tagore belongs unquestionably to Bengali literature but he belongs to Indo-English literature too—indeed he belongs to entire India and the whole world. Tagore was awarded the Nobel Prize for Literature in 1913. Mulk Raj Anand has designated Tagore as the first novelist of India. He feels that Tagore, more than Bankim Chandra Chatterjee could be hailed as the father of modern Indian novel in terms of both theme and technique.

In the twentieth century, National awakening and political uprising gave a great impetus to the Indian novel. The nineteen thirties and forties are the most flourishing decades in the history of Indo-English fiction. Eminent writers like Tagore, Raja Rao, R.K. Narayan, Mulk Raj Anand, Manohar Malgonkar and Abbas identified themselves with the aspirations of their compatriots and portrayed various phases of India's struggle for freedom through their fiction.

Against this brief historical, social and literary background of America and India we find that for writers from both the countries, the bitterness and disbelief which the war had taught was the only tradition. Writers like Hemingway, Dos Passos and others had been uprooted from the secure world of their childhood and plunged into the Western front, the "enormous room" of war. Writers like Tagore, Anand, Abbas and others wrote on the theme of war, revolution and civil strife in India. Thus humanity uprooted, mutilated and massacred was splashed in American as well as Indo-English fiction of the early decades of the twentieth century.

During the 1920's the spiritual and cultural values of Western civilisation had been irreparably damaged. The first of American novels, *This Side of Paradise* (1920) written by Fitzgerald conveys disillusionment and consequent frustration of post-war American youths. Youth was a time for aspiration, passion and desire, but all these emotions were on the decline in war-ravaged West. Men wanted to live but did not know how to fit in a chaotic world. Alienation and disillusionment were the key words of that period.

Dos Passos communicated the actual experience of the war in his novels, particularly in *Three Soldiers* (1921). The devastating effect of the war, crippled the character of John Andrews, a talented musician. His whole individuality was lost in the war mayhem. Cummings' *The Enormous Room* (1921) is a literary account of his imprisonment in France. *The Enormous Room* exposes the hypocrisy and brutality of war. Hemingway's *Moveable Feast* written between 1957 and 1960 also recounts the trauma of the 1920's. The characters of Hemingway's major works are desperate men and women who are living in post-war disillusionment. Violence and war have given them a permanent feeling of insecurity.

In Faulkner's first novel *Soldier's Pay* (1926) the dreadful reality of war is extensively conveyed. The illusion of heroism sent young men to the battlefield but when faced with the brutal reality they ended in the figure of a war hero.

Fitzgerald's *The Great Gatsby* (1925) immediately won praise from distinguished authors like Stein, Wharton, Eliot and others. Like his contemporaries Fitzgerald was fascinated by what had become of the great American Dream. The Dream had been degraded. The impact of World War I on Fitzgerald was tremendous. Using what he knew of post-war America, he dramatised the dreams and illusions of Americans. He focussed upon personal experience which was itself a microcosm of the experience of his nation. The action in *The Great Gatsby* takes place in the wasteland. The valley of ashes symbolises the human situation in an age of chaos. In this desolate area ash gray men drifted here and there unrestfully.

In India too, the early twentieth century was a period of political instability, war and violence. In such fast changing times it was difficult for any writer to live in isolation from what was happening around him. In this period the novel was fast becoming a mirror of the crisis in contemporary life. In the *Journal of Indian Writing in English*, Mulk Raj Anand writes, "I believe literature, though universally significant, deals with contemporary situation. I mean the human and moral situation at any one given time. The writer brings his comprehension of the meaning of life and death into his work by the sheer intensity of his feeling."[1]

The novel is the most important literary form in the twentieth century. Indian writers have shown an amazing sense of kinship with their counterparts in Europe, America and England. Freedom struggle movement, Partition and other political, social and economic changes are the usual themes of Indo-English fiction.

Bankim Chandra Chatterjee (1834-94) was the first Indo-English novelist. His first novel *Raj Mohan's Wife* (1864) was followed by *Anand Math* (1882). Indian nationalism, patriotism caught the attention of creative writers like Tagore, Raja Rao and Anand. These authors started focussing attention on contemporary issues. The novelists became conscious of the reality of man with his surroundings and the changes that were taking place around him. The writers portrayed effectively and realistically the effects these changes had in India. Apart from political issues, another important theme was the East-West conflict.

Coming to Indian novelists, Tagore's *The Home and the World* (1916) and *Four Chapters* (1934) present the political and revolutionary movements of the twentieth century. Mulk Raj Anand's *The Sword and the Sickle* (1942) and K.A. Abbas's *Inquilab* (1955) cover the politics of the twenties. Khushwant Singh's *Train to Pakistan* (1956) recounts the horror of Partition. Similar accounts can be seen in Balchandra Rajan's *The Dark Dancer* (1959), and Manohar Malgonkar's *Distant Drum* (1960) and *A Bend in the Ganges* (1964).

Mulk Raj Anand's (1905-) characters were reflections of the real people he had known during his childhood and youth. His father served in the Indian Army and Anand's early friends inspired him to interpret their lives and transform them to heroes of his first novels. Anand had seen his heroes as pieces of trembling humanity and decided to put them in his books.

Anand suffered an emotional breakdown when the Nazi's killed his close friend, Gertrude Mitchell. He wanted to take revenge for her killing and decided to go to Spain to fight in the war. He went to the war as a volunteer but fainted on the battlefield on the first day itself. There was so much blood lying around that he couldn't take it at all. He had to be hospitalised. He kept thinking of Gertrude and finally recovered after he wrote *Across the Backwaters* (1940) partly on her, partly on the war. Anand's *The Sword and the Sickle* (1942) covers the politics of the twenties. Rivalry and the revolution form the content of this novel.

Manohar Malgonkar (1913-) was a shikari and soldier before he ventured in the profession of writing. He earned his living as a shikari. Later he joined the Indian Army. He had a fairly successful career as a soldier and rose to the rank of Lieutenant Colonel. His first novel *Distant Drum* (1960) was about the Army and the Burma war in which Malgonkar participated. In *Distant Drum* the veil is lifted from what happened in the Partition days in Delhi and later in Kashmir.

A Bend in the Ganges (1964) is an internationally acclaimed best selling novel of massive violence and turbulence that shook the Indian subcontinent at the time of India's freedom struggle. The action ranges from domestic to national bloodshed.

Tagore's name is outstanding as he was one of the writers who first gained for India a place in the world literary scene. Tagore was a musician, painter, educationist, reformer, philosopher, a novelist and a critic of life and literature. He was born on 6th May 1861. Unique among his writing are *Malchanda, Chaturanga* and *Char Adhyaya. Char Adhyaya* (1934) translated in English in 1950 by Surendranath Tagore belongs to the last phase of Tagore's career. *Four Chapters* is remarkable for its contemporaneous quality. Returning after a lapse of eighteen years to the theme of *The Home and the World*, Tagore delivers in *Four Chapters* a further indictment on political fanaticism. Tagore has explained that *Four Chapters* is a love story though it has a political background. S.S. Iyer has compared *Four Chapters* to Shakespeare's *Romeo and Juliet* and Pasternak's *Dr. Zhivago* (1958). Yuri and Lara of *Dr. Zhivago* and Atin and Ela of *Four Chapters* remind one of Henry and Catherine of Hemingway's *Farewell to Arms* (1929). All these are doomed lovers, trapped in the political instability of their times. All these three novels are a gesture of protest, but also a benediction, born of compassion and love.

Let us now turn our attention to Hemingway's *The Old Man and the Sea*, which has rightly been called a classic. It is a work of supreme excellence in every respect. It is a classic in its structure, character portrayal, realism, vision of life and style. The novel is reminiscent of ancient epics. It is much in the spirit of Greek tragedies in which man fights against odds and wins a moral victory. The hero may fail, but he attains an impressive stature by his titanic resistance. *The Old Man and the Sea* is an epic account of Santiago's struggle against the forces of nature. The novel was published in 1952 and in 1953 Hemingway won the Pulitzer Prize for it.

"Often one would acquire a great deal of information about a foreign literature along with a comparatively slender acquaintance of one's own."[2] These are the words of Santha Rama Rau. Earlier in the paper it has been mentioned that after Tagore won the Nobel Prize for Literature he acquired international audience. He was however a rarity. Few Indian authors working in their own provincial languages have managed to reach the wider audience that working in English or the translation of their work can attract. One of these writers whose tone is distinctive and crystal clear is T.S. Pillai. His contribution to Malayalam literature has been tremendous. Thakazhi's *Chemmeen* (1956) translated into English by V.K. Naranayan Menon became the most widely discussed novel of the day. It won Thakazhi the President's Award, the most coveted literary honour in India. Thakazhi, with his moving simplicity of a classic tale *Chemmeen* unfolds the story of devotion, greed and sacrifice, of a taboo violated and of retribution. It is a book that deals with eternal values, and its immemorial rhythms of sea and sky, stir our hearts with their haunting sweetness. *Chemmeen* has the quality of a fable in which the lives, the inner beliefs, the traditions and the sufferings of the community of fishermen are portrayed as a way of life, with a deep and significant moral. *Chemmeen* is a poignant record of the life of seafaring folk on the coast of Alleppey, fringing the Arabian Sea. The peril, heroism, fatality and humanity of the fishermen-folks life is brought out with a vividness, a sense of mounting crisis, and the tremors of tragedy often remind us of Hemingway's *The Old Man and the Sea.*

Both the novels *Chemmeen* and *The Old Man and the Sea* strongly assert that the great thing is not victory but the struggle. In the last section of *Chemmeen*, Palani baited a big shark. The moment it was baited the shark struck hard. The sea churned and the water splashed upward into the sky. Soon Palani was caught in a terrible whirlpool and the shark also pulled the boat with the speed of wind. Finally the fury of the storm increased. Palani fought it bravely, but a huge wave came rolling and his boat got caught up in the whirlpool and sank like a stone.

The last section of *The Old Man and the Sea* deals with Santiago's fierce battle with the sharks. In such a situation, Santiago does not lose heart or expresses helplessness or despair. At the end of the magnificent battle Santiago is defeated but due to his undaunted spirit he remains undefeated.

Hemingway's realism is at its best in *The Old Man and the Sea*. Not only the human characters, but the marlin, the green turtles, the sharks are all vividly described. Such an accurate description is the evidence of the author's first-hand knowledge of the sea and its creatures. The account of the sea-life coming to life at dawn is one of the most impressive passages in the story.

Thakazhi, too, is known as a stark realist. He tempers his realism in *Chemmeen* with a new romanticism. Thakazhi went to middle school at Ambalapuzha. The school was right in the middle of the fishermen's community. Later when he worked as a lawyer, he had many fishermen as clients. The characters like Pareekutty and Karuthamma are thus the real figures he met and knew. In *Chemmeen* too, the description of the fishing boats leaving in the early hours of the morning, some three hours before sunrise is described realistically.

Hemingway's *The Old Man and the Sea* is the climax of Hemingway's long search for disengagement from the social world and to enter the natural world. In *Chemmeen*, Palani was an orphan, he had no memories of his parents. He was the son of the waterfront, not of any home. No one ever cared for him. Circumstances compelled his wife Karuthamma to admit that she did love Pareekutti. That day Palani escaped from society into the natural world. "He had entered a new world. The wide blue expanse of the sea was bathed in silver moonlight."[3] The sea roared with its anger against the poor fisherman, Palani knew how to join forces with a storm. He had sailed the boat in the darkest of dark nights. The storm in the thunder and lighting joined together in the destruction. Clinging to his boat Palani wondered if the merciless slaughter would ever end. The end came only with Palani's death. Thus the classic tales of *The Old Man and the Sea* and *Chemmeen* are superb in all respects. Thakazhi S. Pillai (1916-1999), the grand old man of Malayalam literature died on 10th April, 1999. The Jnanpith Award Winner strode the Malayalam literary scene like a colossus for over five decades. Thakazhi achieved world-wide fame as a humanist writer. Words cannot measure the extraordinary contribution of these authors of international eminence. Their world-wide acclaim proves that great writers like their great works are immortal. From this forum I pay homage to them.

Thus, a comparison of American and Indo-English literature of the early decades of the twentieth century has been a rewarding enterprise. American literature and Indo-English literature are inexhaustible treasure houses of literary gems. One has to dive deep in this literary ocean to explore and appreciate the rare combination of genius and beauty.

REFERENCES

1. Anand, Mulk Raj. "Trends in the Modern Indian Novel," *The Journal of Indian Writing in English* Vol. I (Jan. 1973) i.
2. Pillai, Thakazhi S. *Chemmeen* (Mumbai: Jaico Publishing House, 1998). Introduction by Santha Rama Rau.
3. Pillai 204.

6

Triumph of the Primitive: A Comparative Study of Saul Bellow's *Henderson the Rain King* and R.K. Narayan's *The Guide*

DIGAMBAR SINGH DEWARI

IT IS true that Saul Bellow's *Henderson the Rain King* (1958) is among the most widely celebrated novels of the world. R.K. Narayan's *The Guide* (1958) which won him the prestigious Sahitya Akademi award is also popular among the Indian as well as the Western readers. *The Guide* is also made into a film. The attendance of Lord Mountbatten and Queen Elizabeth at the premiere of the film version of *The Guide* evidences its immediate popularity among the readers.

A common theme seems to underline *Henderson the Rain King* and *The Guide*. The objective of this paper is to analyse critically these two novels with special reference to their thematic aspect. However, on symbolic level, too, these novels embody a close parallel.

There is an unknown voice in Henderson that always says, "I want, I want." But this unknown voice in Henderson is not obviously for money and sex as he himself makes it clear in the opening pages of the novel. The pain of this unknown voice becomes extremely unbearable to Henderson:

> Now I have already mentioned that there was a disturbance in my heart, a voice that spoke there and said, I want, I want, I want! It happened every afternoon, and

> when I tried to suppress it, it got even stronger. It only said one thing, I want, I want! (*HRK*, 23)

The voice in Henderson becomes almost an obsession and occurs at least eighteen times in the novel (*HRK*, 13, 15, 16, 23, 24, 27, 30, 40, 58, 69, 72, 146, 168, 186, 206, 207, 253, 263). But as the narrative progresses, Henderson is made to realise that voice steadily.

There is a constant reference to the phrase "the spirit's sleep" which runs as a corollary to the voice "I want, I want." The phrase "spirit's sleep" also occurs several times in the novel (*HRK*, 61, 69, 91, 142, 188, 290, 296). And like the voice "I want, I want," the phrase "spirit's sleep" also records a steady progress towards Henderson's transformation.

Quite remarkably, Henderson's interview with Willatale, the queen of the Arnewi, serves as a remedy for his agonising voice during his stay with the Arnewi. He is moved by the queen greatly. He tells prince Itelo in appreciation of the queen:

> Now please tell the queen for me, friend, that it does wonderful things for me simply to see her. I don't know whether it's her general appearance or the lion skin or what I feel emanating from her—anyway, it puts my soul at rest (*HRK*, 72-73).

Queen Willatale teaches Henderson "Grun-tu-molani" meaning "you want to live." The impact of "Grun-tu-molani" is so powerful on Henderson that he is highly obliged to the queen and makes constant references to her throughout the novel. The term "Grun-tu-molani" occurs at least fourteen times in the novel with special reference to the queen, her generosity to instruct Henderson and Henderson's regret over his incomplete lessons on "Grun-tu-molani" (*HRK*, 76, 78, 84, 88, 100, 118, 150, 168, 171, 188, 193, 206, 238, 251). But Henderson cannot complete his lessons on "Grun-tu-molani." He blows out the only cistern of the Arnewi in the very process of killing the frogs lying in it. Out of shame Henderson leaves the Arnewi for the Wariri.

As Henderson is obsessed with an inner voice, saying, "I want, I want," in *Henderson the Rain King*, Raju, in *The Guide* is also haunted with a strong passion for Rosie, Marco's wife, and wealth. Raju's passion for Rosie is ever on increase, "I was obsessed with thoughts of Rosie" (*TG*, 115). He speaks of Rosie as if she were his wife, "This woman who had been in my arms forty-eight hours ago was showing off" (*TG*, 135-36).

The obsessed voice in Henderson leads him to blow the cistern of the Arnewi. It also enables him later to lift the wooden statue of Mummah. King Dahfu tells Henderson, "How much better I can interpret now why you succeeded with Mummah. Solely on the basis of that imprisoned want" (*HRK*, 207). Similarly, Raju's passion for wealth, enabling him to earn a huge wealth is evident from Rosie's words:

> What is one to do with so much? All day long and all through the week you are collecting cheques, and more and more often. But when is the time coming when we can enjoy the use of those cheques? (*TG*, 194).

Henderson's obsessed voice and his incomplete lessons on "Grun-tu-molani" lead him to Dahfu, the king of Wariri. Henderson is confident of learning from King Dahfu what he couldn't learn from Queen Willatale completely, "However, under the light of King Dahfu's eyes I comprehended that in bombing the cistern I had not lost my last chance. No sir. By no means" (*HRK*, 149). In a similar vein, Raju's passion for wealth and Rosie, teaches him a lot. Raju cannot resist his temptation for Rosie's jewellery, devised as a trick to involve Raju in a case of forgery by Marco. Raju realises that the forgotten husband cannot be duped thoroughly. For Rosie's sake, Raju drives his mother out of the house. But Rosie leaves him eventually. All these radical events lead Raju to a great realisation. Besides, Raju's imprisonment for two years also transforms him partially. But the complete transformation of Raju is brought through Velan, a villager, who wipes away from Raju's mind even the very desire for food.

In *Henderson the Rain King* Henderson's very entrance to the Wariri village ensures his transformation. Henderson is perpetually exposed to the scenes of fear and death. He is welcomed by the Wariri tribesmen with guns, aimed at him. He is also exposed to a corpse in a hut at night. Henderson's encounter with the corpse in the hut at night is devised to test his courage and strength. Henderson is shown human skulls, lying in a large wooden bowl and corpses hanging within the Wariri village. Henderson deserves victory's crown when he succeeds to lift Mummah. But he receives sheer humiliation. His clothes are stripped, he is whipped and thrown into mud. But Henderson's real training towards his transformation starts as an apprentice to King Dahfu. King Dahfu exposes Henderson to the lioness repeatedly. Similarly, in *The Guide*, Raju's apprenticeship as a saint to Velan begins the very moment Raju feigns sainthood before Velan, in a temple after his release from the prison. Raju is forced to continue this feigned sainthood till he falls a victim to his own pedantry.

King Dahfu initiates Henderson into his transformation through lion-therapy. The very sight of the lioness unnerves Henderson. Therefore, King Dahfu advises Henderson to advance the lioness, "closer—little by little" (*HRK*, 196). Henderson is made to observe the lioness, appreciate her beauty, contemplate her, absorb lion qualities, imitate or dramatise the behaviour of lions. He is made to be the lion, feel the lion, lower on the forepaws and roar.

In a different way, Raju in *The Guide* is initiated into true sainthood by Velan through a spiritual-therapy. Despite his sinful life, Raju is expected to perform like a saint to end drought. He is made to go everyday to the river's edge, face the river's source and stand in knee-deep water from six to eight in the morning, muttering something between his lips. Then Raju would go back and lie down on a mat in the pillared hall of the temple and contemplate there all the time. Raju is forced to observe a fasting. Raju confides his sinful existence to Velan to avoid his ordeal. But Velan still addresses Raju as "Swami" with the same vehemence. This he does purposely to let Raju listen to his inner voice and become a saint while performing the role of a saint. To quote Fakrul Alam in this context: "It may be in the nature of things for villagers like Velan to apotheosise Raju-types...."[1]

The lion-therapy for Henderson as King Dahfu feels is inevitable for Henderson's transformation:

> First she is unavoidable. Test it, and you will find she is unavoidable. And this is what you need as you are an avoider. Oh, you have accomplished momentous avoidances. But she will change that. She will make consciousness to shine. She will burnish you. She will force the present moment upon you (*HRK*, 230).

As in *Henderson the Rain King*, Henderson, out of fear avoids his sessions on lion-therapy at the initial stage, Raju in *The Guide*, too avoids his fasting for the first three days of his imposed fasting. On the first day of his fasting he manages to eat stale food, left over from the previous day. On the second and third day of his fasting he still remains obsessed with the thoughts of food. Raju can no longer avoid fasting. He is moved by the faith, Velan has placed in him. So he resolves to fast sincerely, "If by avoiding food I should help the trees bloom, and the grass grow, why not do it thoroughly?" (*TG*, 237-38).

As the lioness is unavoidable, Henderson begins to take his sessions with her seriously. He dramatises the behaviour of the lioness. In this very process of dramatising the behaviour of the lioness, Henderson assumes himself as the beast:

> And so I was the beast. I gave myself to it, and all my sorrow came out in the roaring. My lungs supplied the air but the note came from my soul. The roaring scalded my throat and hurt the corners of my mouth and presently I filled the den like a bass organ pipe. This was where my heart had sent me, with its clamour. This is where I ended up. Oh, Nebuchadnezzar! How well I understand that prophecy of Daniel. For I had claws, and hair, and some teeth, and I was bursting with hot noise, but when all this had come forth, there was still a remainder. That last thing of all was my human longing (*HRK*, 236-37).

The impact of this therapy on Henderson is miraculously wonderful. Henderson discards his original name, E.H.

Henderson and wants to enrol himself at Medical Centre as "Leo E. Henderson" (*HRK*, 252). But Henderson's human longing is fulfilled in Newfoundland when he shows a lion-cub (containing the spirit of Dahfu), to an orphan child and adopts him. That Henderson attains a complete transformation, eventually, is supported by Philip Toynbee, when he says that Henderson "returns to America with a symbolical lion-cub and the sense that he has been spiritually renewed."[2]

Quite in conformity with Henderson's lion-therapy, Raju's fasting also culminates in Raju's transformation. Raju's determination to avoid food gives him a peculiar floating feeling, "This enjoyment is something Velan cannot take away from me" (*TG*, 238). Like Henderson, Raju is also transformed eventually. On eleventh day of his fasting Raju brings rain and dies instantly. But Raju's death is only a transformation of his life. To quote C.D. Narasimhaiah: "Raju's death, viewed symbolically, means that the individual by losing his life in water brings rain (and life) to his fellowmen, and his death, a 'death by water' is really not death but a means of self-purification and self-realisation."[3]

Apart from thematic similarity there also exist other similarities in *Henderson the Rain King* and *The Guide*. For example, people in both the novels suffer immeasurably from severe drought. In both the novels cattle die of drought. In *Henderson the Rain King* the portrayal of a cow passing away and the owner begging the cow not to leave him is full of pathos. However, the Arnewi have a frog-infested cistern that contains sufficient water. But the Arnewi consider frog as a taboo animal. So they don't allow their cattle to drink this contaminated water of the cistern. In *The Guide* the drought causes death of a buffalo. A little later more cattle are found dead here and there. The drought situation in *The Guide* is described realistically at length. It covers a detailed account of the overall damage caused by the drought.

Moreover, the rain bringing ceremony, presented realistically in a seriocomic vein, lends charm and vitality to *Henderson the Rain King* and *The Guide* as well. Besides, it is presented in an occult tradition in both the novels. This ceremony lasts several hours on a certain day in *Henderson the Rain King*. But in *The Guide* it cover twenty hours, two hours everyday in the morning. The ceremony in *The Guide* is ritualistic. The outstanding features of the rain bringing ceremony in *Henderson the Rain King* are—a huge mob, most of the people being naked, painted and gaudy, screams and shouts of the people, salutes of the amazons in honour of the king, king's late father, Gmilo, for Henderson and others, deep bloody cuts on the chest of a grinning face, grand salute of the guns, throwing of skulls, sacrifices of the cattle, stripping the idols of gods disrespectfully, lift of the idols of gods, Henderson's success to lift Mummah, Henderson hailed as the Rain King, the humiliation of Henderson, thought by the Wariri as an essential act to bring the required rain. Raju in *The Guide* is required to go to the river's edge, face its source, stand knee-deep in the water from six to eight in the morning, mutter something between his lips, shut his eyes, press his palms together in a salute to the gods, presumably, to perform his ritual daily. Raju's penance also brings in a huge mob and a lot of activity in and around the temple. But the mob contributes less significantly to the bringing of rain.

It is quite interesting to note that the ordeal Henderson and Raju put themselves to, in order to bring rain, carries an ironic implication with reference to their knowledge or invention. Henderson's account of the flowers, he had read in a magazine before he left home, sounds mythical. Henderson tells that these flowers bloom in the desert once in forty or fifty years. A bucket of water fails to germinate the seeds of these flowers. These seeds need a heavy rainfall, "It has to be the rain coming through the soil" (*HRK*, 207). This mythical story, symbolically, proves true when Henderson succeeds to bring a deluge through an equally mythical rain bringing ceremony. The rare and difficult life of the flowers refers obliquely to the austere and occult ceremony that brings the required rain. Similarly, the story narrated by Raju to the villagers about a penance ever made by a holy man to bring rain, ironically, proves true later through Raju himself.

Further, animal imagery abounds both in *Henderson the Rain King* and *The Guide*. The animal imagery in *Henderson the Rain King* ranges from bear to pig to cow to frog to lion. The images of two animals—cobra and crocodile, figure quite significantly in *The Guide*. These images of animal in both the novels help the reader to analyse and appreciate the novels thoroughly. For example, Henderson as a raiser of pigs proclaims himself as a bum and thinks of himself as a pig. Later his sessions on lion-therapy under the directions of King Dahfu enable him to absorb lion-like qualities. Similarly, the image of cobra associated with Rosie, and Raju's association with Rosie, enables the reader justify the prosperity that Raju and Rosie gain through the strenuous dance-shows. The cobra, K. Chellappan maintains is a "symbol of primordial energy."[4] Similarly, crocodile is an archetypal image of hypocrisy. The feigned sainthood of Raju is externalised in the image of crocodile which remains "almost a myth" (*TG*, 237). Later the crocodile dies in the novel. The death of crocodile symbolises the death of Raju's feigned sainthood for it coincides with a crucial event in Raju's life. Raju casts away the very mask of sainthood and undertakes his penance selflessly for the benefit of humanity.

Henderson the Rain King and *The Guide* both allow an ample scope for their heroes to undergo a steady progression in their lives. For example, Henderson, the pig raiser, becomes "Sungo, the Rain King" when he lifts Mummah. After the death of Dahfu, Henderson becomes Roi Henderson, Yassi Henderson. Similarly, Raju, from his job of a tourist guide, becomes an impresario to Nalini (Rosie), and later, a prisoner. After his release from prison, Raju becomes a saint and concludes his life as a martyr.

In *Henderson the Rain King*, Saul Bellow uses the fragments of a number of Western myths. He uses the familiar rituals of quest and initiation from a comic perspective to lay bare the reality. Henderson's journey into the mythical and remote villages of Africa to find out the real meaning of his life and Henderson's return to America as a spiritually renewed man, affirm that even the remote villages of Africa are capable of training and reforming a civilised man of America. Similarly, by using Valmiki myth in *The Guide*, R.K. Narayan strips the layers of unreality from Raju (the guide) by placing him ironically under the guidance of Velan, a village peasant.

REFERENCES

Alam, Fakrul. "Narrative Strategies in Two Narayan Novels," *R.K. Narayan: Critical Perspectives*, ed. A.L. McLeod (New Delhi: Sterling Publishers Pvt. Ltd., 1994), 19.

Toynbee, Philip. "Saul Bellow," *Encounter*, 13, No. 3, (1959), 69.

Narasimhaiah, C.D. "R.K. Narayan's *The Guide*," *Aspects of Indian Writing in English*, ed. M.K. Naik (New Delhi: Macmillan, 1979), 198.

Chellappan, K. "The Dialectics of Myth and Irony in R.K. Narayan," *R.K. Narayan: Critical Perspectives*, ed. A.L. McLeod (New Delhi: Sterling Pulishers Pvt. Ltd., 1994), 28.

WORKS CITED

Bellow, Saul. *Henderson the Rain King*, (1958; rpt. New York: Popular Library, 1963). Cited as *HRK*.

Narayan, R.K. *The Guide* (1958; rpt. Madras: Indian Thought Publications, 1995). Cited as *TG*.

7

The Pilgrimage of Siddhartha: A Quest for Truth, Vision and Wisdom

P.C. PRADHAN

I

THIS IS a strange world with its strange course of actions and designs. Very often, we are greatly perturbed when we think of the go of the creation. It is really very difficult on our part to comprehend the basic objectives of such an immanent universe which seems to be incomprehensible and mysterious. Theory gives a systematic base to comprehension and practice. But the validity of a theory can only be verified through practical implementation of the ideas contained in it. In regards to life and *Sansar* experience is the only way to wisdom. Knowledge about the *Sansar* is not *Sansar*, the experience really leads us to wisdom which can be verified by truth and vision. Visionary glimpses about life are sometimes important. However, without the real experience in connection with these visionary glimpses, we cannot attain true wisdom. At best they can help us acquire some knowledge that may be an attribute of our mind having no definite assimilation in our blood, which is the real element of having connection with experience. Hermann Hesse's novel *Siddhartha* is about Siddhartha's pilgrimage for a spiritual quest to have the experience of wisdom. In Hesse's *Siddhartha,* we perceive that Siddhartha was on a pilgrimage abandoning the pleasures of youth hoping to be absorbed in holy spiritual life. In the process, he had rather turned into a life of flesh rejecting the life of contemplation. As the father of his motherless spoilt son and expecting to reform him, he is otherwise lost in despair. However, he begins a new life smelling the truth in the sound of the running water of the river where he begins to understand and experience what real "wisdom" is.

Siddhartha attains wisdom through his pilgrimage, through his wandering, through his experience of travelling not only through the varieties of land but also travelling through the varieties of life. Bacon has rightly said: "Travel, in the younger sort, is a part of education; in the elder, a part of experience" (Sinha 11), Pilgrimage makes a man more experienced and mature. Here Belloc's statements are worth-quoting: "A pilgrimage is, of course, an expedition to some venerated place to which a vivid memory of sacred things experienced or a long and wonderful history of human experience in divine matters, or a personal attraction affecting the soul impels one" (Sinha 112). The essence and goal of pilgrimage is the purification of the soul of a being. "A pilgrimage ought to be nothing but a nobler kind of travel" (Belloc in Sinha 113). Belloc further argues that pilgrimage brings out a "human satisfaction of a need, the fulfilling of an instinct in us, the realisation of the imagined horizons, the reaching of a goal" (Sinha 114). The pilgrim should be "humble and devout, human and charitable" (Belloc 115) and he should have the attitude to appreciate and understand this great world and its people in their interrelationships. The best way of undertaking a pilgrimage is on foot "where one is man like any other man, with the sky above one, and the road beneath, and the world on every side, and time to see all" (Belloc in Sinha 115). Siddhartha has chosen the best way of pilgrimage by walking on foot and having time to think and see everything. Seeing is his experience, his vision, his wisdom, his realisation of the Truth. His travelling is both physical and mental and consequently really spiritual.

II

Siddhartha, the *Brahmin's* handsome son was intelligent and thirsty for knowledge. He grew up with his friend, Govinda in his village. He had already mastered a major portion of vedic knowledge and *Brahmin* rituals. His father was happy to see "him growing up to be a great learned man, a priest, a prince among the *Brahmins*" (Hesse 3). His mother was proud to see her son, Siddhartha—"strong, handsome supple-limbed, greeting her with complete grace" (4). The *Brahmins'* young daughters pined for Siddhartha's love when he "walked through the streets of the town, with his lofty brow, his king-like eyes and his slim figure" (4). Govinda, Siddhartha's friend, loved him in all respects especially for "his intellect, his fine ardent thoughts, his strong will, his high vocation" (4). He wanted to follow his beloved Siddhartha "as his friend, his companion, his servant, his lance-bearer, his shadow" (4). Despite the fact that he made everybody happy, he himself had "no joy in his heart" (4). "Dreams and restless thoughts came flowing to him from the river, from the twinkling stars at night, from the sun's melting rays. Dreams and a restlessness of the soul came to him, arising from the smoke of the sacrifices, emanating from the verses of the *Rig-Veda,* trickling through from the teachings of the old *Brahmins*" (4). Siddhartha felt that he could not get peace in his present set-up. A volley of questions stirred his mind and heart regarding "Creation," "*Atman*," "Self" and so on. Above all the question of "existence of self" disturbed him the most:

> But where was this self, this innermost? It was not flesh and bone, it was not thought or consciousness. That was what the wise man taught. Where, then, was it? To press towards the Self, towards *Atman*—was there another way that was worth seeking? Nobody showed the way, nobody knew it—neither his father, nor the teachers and wise men, nor the holy songs. The *Brahmins* and their holy books knew everything: They had gone into everything—the creation of the world, the origin of speech, food, inhalation, exhalation, the arrangement of the senses, the acts of the gods. They knew a tremendous number of things—but was it worthwhile knowing all these things if they did not know the one important thing, the only important thing? (5-6).

That is how Siddhartha was greatly perturbed. He felt that no *Brahmin* attained peace and salvation though they were well-versed with the *Vedas* and *Upanishadas.* Though this *Brahmin* community had noble thoughts, still they could not verify the concept of the *Upanishadas* of *Sama-veda*: "Your soul is the whole world" (6). All learned and wise *Brahmins* including his father didn't attain "*Atman* in sleep" (6). He was in doubt if his father had "*Atman*" in him. This thought made Siddhartha sorrow-stricken and hence he felt: "One must find the source within one's Self, one must possess it. Everything else was seeking-a detour, error" (6). Possessed by an eternal thirst for knowledge, Siddhartha often repeated the following words from the *Chandogya-upanishads:* "In truth, the name of the *Brahman* is *Satyam.* Indeed, he who knows it enters the heavenly world each day" (7). Being unable to attain peace along with his friend Govinda, Siddhartha sat under the banyan tree and recited: "*Om* is the bow, the arrow is the soul/ *Brahman* is the arrow's goal/ At which one aims unflinchingly" (7). Soon after the meditation Siddhartha decided to be an ascetic and leave home. Against the will of his father, though he got his permission, Siddhartha left home for the life of a pilgrim in search of *Atman,* peace and salvation. With him joined his shadow, Govinda.

In the evening of the day of their departure, the two friends were accepted by the *Samans* on their request to learn lessons from them by leading the life of theirs. Without taking care of their sensual pleasure, the two new *Samans* wanted to conquer hunger, thirst and senses. In the process Siddhartha had long nails "on his thin fingers and a dry, bristly beard" (11) on his chin. "His glance became icy when he encountered women; his lips curled with contempt when he passed a town of well-dressed people" (11). On the whole, he resented materialism: "they were all illusions of sense, happiness and beauty. All were doomed to decay. The world tasted bitter. Life was pain" (11). Siddhartha became indulgent in hard penance with the sole goal of becoming "empty of thirst, desire, dreams, pleasure and sorrow—to let the Self die" (12) and attain peace, the *Nirvana* of the soul.

Therefore he "practised self-denial and meditation according to the *Saman* rules" as per the instructions of the eldest *Saman*. In the *Srimad Bhagavad Gita,* Arjuna is taught by the Lord about meditation and control of mind in *Adhyaya* II (*slokas* 60-63, 67, 14, 15, 38), *Adhyaya* III (*slokas* 36-41), *Adhyaya* V (*slokas* 22-24, 26, 28), *Adhyaya* VI (*slokas* 3-7, 10-14, 16, 17, 19, 24-27), *Adhyaya* XII (*slokas* 13-19), *Adhyaya* XIV (*slokas* 22-25), *Adhyaya* XVI (*slokas* 21, 22) and *Adhyaya* XVIII (*slokas* 36, 37). Mind is to be controlled and death of desire is necessary for selfless performance of work. Control of mind will be followed by detachment from indulgence in materialism: "If the mind is not carefully guarded, desire will find its perch in the senses, seize our thoughts, pollute our intelligence and finally ruin us. Therefore the battle must be fought with desire at the gate, even while it seeks entrance in our thoughts" (Rajagopalachari 59). N.S. Subramaniam interprets the *Gita* and writes: "When one is rid of desires, is bereft of attachment to the sense-objects and sense-organs, is free from the cravings for enjoyment, when his mind in self-control rests easily on the Self (*Atman*)—then such a one with a spirit of renunciation too, is said to have attained *yoga*" (63). True happiness springs from the serenity of the mind of the *yogi* whose soul "is liberated even though it is still imprisoned in the flesh" (Rajagopalachari 65). The person who controls the senses and remains himself aloof from material pleasures attains a blissful soul, peace, serenity of mind and "a steady wisdom" (Vireswarananda 76). Siddhartha learned many things from the *Samans*; but he could not attain his goal—the attainment of peace and *Nirvana*:

> ...he learned many ways of losing the Self. He travelled along the path of self-denial through pain, through voluntary suffering and conquering of pain, through hunger, thirst and fatigue. He travelled the way of self-denial through meditation through the emptying of the mind of all images. Along these and other paths did he learn to travel. He lost his Self a thousand times and for days on end he dwelt in no-being. But although the paths took him away from Self, in the end they always led back to it. Although Siddhartha fled from Self a thousand times

> dwelt in nothing, dwelt in animal and stone, the return was inevitable, the hour was inevitable when he would again find himself in sunshine or in moonlight, in shadow or in rain, and was again Self and Siddhartha, again felt the torment of the onerous life cycle (Hesse 13).

So there was disillusion in Siddhartha in a *Saman's* way of life. On their way to begging, Siddhartha asks his friend Govinda, "Do you think we are any further? Have we reached our goal?" (13). Though Govinda was optimistic about their moving in "a spiral path" (15) towards salvation Siddhartha was rather arguing that they were moving in a cyclic path. He, therefore, told his friend in sorrow: "I suffer thirst, Govinda and on this long *Saman* path my thirst has not grown less. I have always thirsted for knowledge, I have always been full of questions" (15-16). But this thirst for learning is detrimental to understand *Atman,* the Self. As such Siddhartha felt to renounce the *Saman* way of living as it was futile to attain *Nirvana* by this way. In the circle of *Samans* both the friends had heard about Gotama, the Illustrious One of Sakyamuni who had vast knowledge and attained *Nirvana* and they decided to leave the *Samans* for Gotama's way of life. Though the eldest of the *Samans* got angry at the beginning to learn of their departure, later on he blessed them and wished them for a good journey (19).

Gotama's favourite abode was the Jetavan grove near the town of Savathi, presented by the rich merchant of Anathapindika. After staying there a night, the two friends saw the Buddha as a monk in yellow cowl "lost in thought" (23). Siddhartha marked that the Buddha with the begging bowl and the secret smile in his face walked along peacefully with all his limbs, gestures and postures radiating peace and completeness and reflecting "a continual quiet, and unfading light, an invulnerable peace" (23). He knew the substance of the Buddha's teachings and hence he never expected to learn from Gotama's teachings. On the other hand he observed Gotama's head, his shoulders, his feet, his still downward hanging hand and every joint of every finger of his hand radiated knowledge and truth. "This man, this Buddha, was truly a holy man to his finger tips.

Never had Siddhartha esteemed a man so much, never had he loved a man so much" (23-24).

After return from the town, the Buddha taught his disciples four main points and Eightfold path. He also talked about suffering, cause of suffering and the way to release from suffering was to go the Buddha way for salvation. Govinda, being swayed by Buddha's teachings paid his allegiance to him. However, Siddhartha did not join the monks' community and bade farewell to Govinda and met Gotama next day for a discussion. He appreciated Gotama's clear convictions and teachings in regards to the coherence of the world "without a loophole" (27). However, as per the teachings of Gotama, "the unity of the world, the coherence of all events, the embracing of the big and the small from the same stream, from the same law of cause, of becoming and dying" (27) clearly emerges. Again according to Gotama's teachings the coherence is broken at one place: "Through a small gap there streams into the world of variety something strange, something new, something that was not there before and that cannot be demonstrated and proved that is your doctrine of rising above the world, of salvation. With this small gap, through this small break, however, the eternal and single world law breaks down again. Forgive if I raise this objection" (27). Listening quietly to Siddhartha's objections, Gotama warned him for his thirst for knowledge and interpreting the conflict of words in a clever manner. Again he viewed that opinions meant little. The real goal of his teachings is salvation from suffering rather than anything else. But Siddhartha argued that Gotama's teachings did not contain the secret of his experience at the time of enlightenment. That is why he wanted to go on his own way—"not to seek another and better doctrine...but to leave all doctrines and all teachers and to reach my goal alone—or die" (28). The Buddha smiled and blessed the *Saman* and again warned him to be on his "guard against too much cleverness" (29). Siddhartha thought: "I also, would like to look and smile, sit and walk like that, so free, so worthy, so restrained, so candid, so childlike and mysterious. A man only looks and walks like that when he has conquered his Self. I also will conquer my Self" (29). Though Siddhartha had great estimation for the Buddha, he had some resentment against him because he had robbed him of his friend, "who believed in me and who now believes in him; he was my shadow and is now Gotama's shadow" (29). However, this Buddha changed the whole path of his pilgrimage by giving him Siddhartha, his Self.

Siddhartha had attained adulthood now. He was no more a youth. On his way from Jetavan, he thought deeply "until he reached a point where he recognised causes, for to recognise causes, it seemed to him, is to think and through thought alone feelings become knowledge and are not lost, but become real and begin to mature" (30). Though the teachers could teach high doctrines, they could not teach individual experience. It is unique for everybody and hence Siddhartha has a Self, which is quite different from others. Therefore, Siddhartha now wants to know about himself, Siddhartha. He would no more fly away from himself; he would not rather destroy his Self. It is futile to seek "the unknown innermost the nucleus of all things, *Atman,* life, the Divine, the Absolute" (31). By doing so he lost himself on the way. He, therefore, decided not to fly away from Siddhartha any more. "The world was beautiful, strange and mysterious" (32). Amongst the beautiful and colourful objects of the world "Siddhartha, the awakened one" (32) is on the way to himself. Meaning and reality are not illusory. They "were not hidden somewhere behind things, they were in them, in all of them" (32). As an awakened Siddhartha he was born afresh to start a new life, completely a new one. He would not return to his father's home. Rather he would lead a lonely life all alone in this vast universe. But he did not lose hope: "...when the world around him melted away, when he stood alone like a star in the heavens, he was overwhelmed by a feeling of icy despair, but he was more firm than ever. That was the last shudder of his awakening, the last pains of birth" (33). Therefore he must face all that comes on his way without any inhibition.

III

The Buddha had enlightenment under the *peepal* trees after he had been disillusioned by doing the *Sansar*. His wisdom came to him after he himself experienced the sorrows and suffering, desires and senses in the world. On the other hand, this Siddhartha traversed from the life of a learned *Brahmin* boy through the *Saman's* way of life to a discussion with the Illustrious One. He feels that he has enlightenment. On his way of pilgrimage "he learned something new on every step of his path" (37). Previously he did never realise that this world was so beautiful and real. "The moon and the stars were beautiful, the brook, the shore, the forest and rock, the goat and the golden beetle, the flower and butterfly were beautiful. It was beautiful and pleasant to go through the world like that, so childlike, so awakened, so concerned with the immediate, without any distrust" (38). Despite the fact that everything existed—hunger and desire, light and shadow, moon and stars—, he had never seen them previously. He now feels this is the world—the real wisdom. He now remembers what he had experienced in the garden of Jetavan in the presence of the Buddha: "...that the Buddha's wisdom and secret was not teachable, that it was inexpressible and incommunicable—and which he had once experienced in an hour of enlightenment was just what he had now set off to experience, what he was now beginning to experience. He must gain experience himself?" (38). For a long time he believed that his Self was *Atman*. It was of the "same eternal nature as *Brahman*, but he had never found his Self because he had wanted to trap it in the net of thoughts" (39). The body is not the Self, nor even the senses, the thought, understanding, acquired wisdom or art by which one can draw conclusions and spin new thoughts. Nothing can be achieved so long as one goes on destroying the "incidental Self" (39) feeding it with "thoughts and erudition" (39). It is imperative and worthwhile upon a being to listen to the voices of both thought and the senses. Through their fusion an "inward voice" is generated in the Self, which is the real Truth about life. That is the experience, the vision, the wisdom. Hence Siddhartha would no more neglect the voice of the senses, because his pursuit of spiritual quest had become futile, incomplete without sensual experiences. Mere knowledge of sensuality is not real sensuality. One must experience sensuality which "is a fulfilment—the great dark knowledge you can't have in your head—the dark involuntary being. It is death to one's self—but it is the coming into being of another" (Lawrence, 46-47). Birkin in the novel *Women in Love* resents the knowledge of sensuality in the head. He pleads that Hermione must experience the "dark knowledge" in her blood. In that sensual experience, there is the liberation of the soul, the "powerful beauty of life" (48). That is why the inward voice at the subconscious level persuades Siddhartha to be guided by the Self, the sensual pleasure being one of the significant components for life to be complete, to be meaningful, to be real, to be earnest to attain wisdom. That is why Siddhartha dreams in the hut of the ferryman:

> Thereupon he embraced Govinda, put his arm round him, and as he drew him to his breast and kissed him, he was Govinda no longer, but a woman and out of the woman's gown emerged a full breast, and Siddhartha lay there and drank; sweet and strong tasted the milk from this breast. It tasted of woman and man, of sun and forest, of animal and flower, of every fruit, of every pleasure. It was intoxicating. When Siddhartha awoke, the pale river shimmered past the door of the hut, and in the forest the cry of an owl rang out, deep and clear (Hesse 40).

No doubt Govinda is Siddhartha's the most intimate friend. But in the dream he sees that Govinda has been transformed into a woman. Siddhartha now desires a woman to feed his sensual hunger, to be intimate with him. That is quite prominent in his dream. Therefore when he parts from his friendly ferryman, he feels that the ferryman is "like Govinda, he thought smiling. All whom I meet on the way are like Govinda" (40). The sensual pleasure is a necessity on everyman's way of pilgrimage. On his way of journey the small children are scared to see him. Near a brook Siddhartha sees a young beautiful woman washing clothes "with her moist lips gleaming attractively in her young face" (41). When Siddhartha asks her the distance of the town, she also exchanges some light remarks asking if the *Samans* are not allowed to sleep with woman at night. She also makes a gesture to Siddhartha inviting him to a kind of enjoyment of love which the holy books call "ascending the tree" (41). The sensual desire in Siddhartha is now stirred:

> Siddhartha felt his blood kindle, and as he recognised his dream again at the moment, he stooped a little towards the woman and kissed the brown tip of her breast. Looking up he saw her face smiling, full of desire, and her half-closed eyes pleading with longing.
>
> Siddhartha also felt a longing and the stir of sex in him but as he had never yet touched a woman, he hesitated a moment although his hands were ready to seize her. At that moment he heard his inward voice and the voice said "No." Then all the magic disappeared from the young woman's smiling face; he saw nothing but the ardent glance of a passionate young woman. Gently he stroked her cheek and quickly disappeared from the disappointed woman into the bamboo wood (41).

Before evening he reached a town where he saw a procession of people, a train of men and women servants moved in the middle of which a young beautiful woman, seated in a sedan chair, was carried by four people. He looked at the lady: "Beneath heaped-up black hair he saw a bright, very sweet, very clever face, a bright red mouth like a freshly cut fig, artful eyebrows painted in a high arch, dark eyes, clever and observant, and a clear slender neck above her green and gold gown. The woman's hands were firm and smooth, long and slender with broad gold bangles on her wrists" (42). Siddhartha was greatly moved by "the bright fair face" and "the clever arched eyes" and gazed at the beautiful courtesan, Kamala for a moment. His heart rejoiced as he bowed low to her. She reciprocated with a smile and disappeared into the mango grove. Next morning Siddhartha got his beard cut, combed his hair and took a bath in the river. In the afternoon he went to meet Kamala, the most beautiful courtesan. He told her that he left the path of a *Saman* and decided not to speak to beautiful woman like Kamala "without lowered eyes" (43). She is the first lady with whom Siddhartha speaks "without lowered eyes." She is rather surprised to know that "a *Saman* from the woods" (44) should come to her and desires to learn from her. It is almost her first experience. Many people including young *Brahmin* sons visit the courtesan with fine clothes, fine shoes, plenty of money and plenty of presents for Kamala. That is, too, the only criterion for Siddhartha to fulfil if he desires to learn the art of love and kisses from her. When Siddhartha enquires if fair Kamala is not "afraid of a *Saman* from the forest, who has come to learn about love" (45), she reproaches him as a stupid ignorant *Saman* living in the forest among the jackals and having no knowledge about women. At this Siddhartha becomes self-conscious and utters:

> 'Oh, the *Samana* is strong and afraid of nothing. He could force you, fair maiden, he could rob you, he could hurt you.'
>
> 'No, *Samana*, I am not afraid. Has a *Samana* or a *Brahmin* ever feared that someone could come and strike him and rob him of his knowledge, of his piety, of his power for depth of thought? No, because they belong to himself, and he can only give exactly how it is with Kamala and with the pleasures of love. Fair and red are Kamala's lips, but try to kiss them against Kamala's will, and not one drop of sweetness will you obtain from them—although they knew well how to give sweetness. You are an apt pupil, Siddhartha, so learn also this. One can beg, buy, be presented with and find love in the streets, but it can never be stolen. You have misunderstood. Yes, it would be a pity if a fine young man like you misunderstood' (45).

Siddhartha is convinced at Kamala's argument and seeks her advice on how to earn money for fine clothes and fine shoes. He knows the art of "thinking, waiting and fasting." He does not know if they would help him for earning money. He also knows how to compose poetry, but he is not sure if Kamala can give a kiss for a poem. After recitation of a poem, Kamala is highly pleased and decides to kiss him:

> She drew him to her with eyes. He put his face against hers, placed his lips against hers, which were like a freshly cut fig. Kamala kissed him deeply, and to Siddhartha's great excitement he felt how much she taught him, how clever she was, how she mastered him, repulsed him, lured him, and how after this long kiss a long series of other kisses, all different awaited him. He stood still, breathing deeply. At that moment he was like a child astonished at the fullness of knowledge and learning which unfolded itself before his eyes (46-47).

Deciding to help the poor *Saman*, Kamala suggests him to meet her there next day as a visitor has come to meet her at the moment. Siddhartha meets Kamala next day and he is informed to meet Kamaswami, the rich merchant of the town to help in his business enterprise and advises him: "I do not want you to be his servant, but his equal, Kamaswami is beginning to grow old and indolent. If you please him, he will place great confidence in you" (48). However Siddhartha is not to accept the fact that he is lucky only for the sake of Kamala. On the other hand he pleads Siddhartha can do things because "he waits, he thinks, he fasts, but he goes through the affairs of the world like the stone through water, without doing anything, without bestirring himself; he is drawn and lets himself fall. He is drawn by his goal, for he does not allow anything to enter his mind which opposes his goal" (49). Kamala is pleased with his argument and adds that Siddhartha can do things because he is a handsome man, because his glance pleases women, that he is lucky" (49). Then Siddhartha kisses her and utters before leaving her: "May it be so, my teacher. May my glance always please you, may good fortune always come to me from you" (50).

Siddhartha met Kamaswami, "a supple, lively man, with greying hair, with clever prudent eyes and a sensual mouth" (51) next day. Kamaswami asked the *Brahmin* if he was in need of service from him; but Siddhartha retorted that he was interested to work on his free will rather than out of necessity. He hated possessions. However after a brief discourse, Kamaswami accepted him to work in his business. Siddhartha learned many things but "was never servile to the merchant, but compelled him as an equal and even more than his equal. Kamaswami conducted his business with care and after with passion, but Siddhartha regarded it all as a game, the rules of which he endeavoured to learn well, but which did not stir his heart" (53). Everyday he visited the beautiful Kamala at the appointed hour with "fine clothes, fine shoes and beautiful presents." He spent wonderful hours with the clever, beautiful courtesan and became her pupil, her lover, her friend. Herewith Kamala lay the real value and meaning of his present life, not with Kamaswami" (54). At the beginning he was rather indifferent to business, he was neither happy at the profit nor sorrowful at the loss. On one occasion he argued with Kamaswami in a very arrogant way: "I have learned from you how much a basket of fish costs and how much interest one can claim for lending money. This is your knowledge. But I did not learn how to think from you, my dear Kamaswami. It would be better if you learned that from me" (56). Siddhartha had no heart in the business. His main objective in business was to earn money for the sake of Kamala. Occasionally the inner voice disturbed him much and he felt that he was "leading a strange life, that he was doing many things that were only a game, that he was quite cheerful and sometimes experiened pleasure, but that real life was flowing past him and did not touch him. Like a player who plays with his ball, he played with his business, with people around him, watched them, derived amusement from them; but with his heart, with his real nature, he was not there. His real Self wandered elsewhere, far away, wandered on and on invisibly and had nothing to do with his life" (57).

This is his distinctive Self, individuality. For a long time he "had lived the life of the world without belonging to it" (60). Siddhartha loved Kamala on the principle of "give-take" basis. Both of them had individuality like the stars. Love creates a bond between man and woman. It is a mystic conjunction "the immediate bond between man and woman" (Lawrence: *Women in Love*, 169). However "love is a freedom together"

(Lawrence 169) like stars. The law of creation is such that "one must commit oneself to a conjunction with the other forever. But it is not selfless—it is a maintaining of the Self in mystic balance and integrity—like a star balanced with another star" (169-70). In love man and woman must be free. "They would give each other this star-equilibrium which alone is freedom" (360). Thus both Siddhartha and Kamala have distinctive individualities even through their conjunction and unison. Kamala is distinctive with "a stillness and sanctuary" which the clever Kamaswami lacks. Siddhartha believed that most people "are like a falling leaf that drifts and turns in the air flutters and falls to the ground" (Hesse 58). This is in sharp contrast to Shelley's concept of a falling leaf in "Ode to the West Wind." Siddhartha is not desirous of being a falling leaf of Shelley which is under the control of the wind and desirous of having the touch of wild, violent West Wind to have a new lease of life, to be liberated: "Oh, lift me as a wave, a leaf, a cloud! I fall upon the thorns of life! I bleed!" (Shelley in Tripathy 30). Siddhartha wants to be the vigorous "Spirit fierce" (Tripathy 30) West Wind which would have the capacity to "drive my dead thoughts over the universe/ like withered leaves to quicken a new birth!" (Shelley in Tripathy 30). Hence Siddhartha wants to be a Siddhartha with all the potentialities of Gotama rather than to be fallen leaves like his disciples to follow him. These people have no wisdom within to guide themselves. Among the people Siddhartha knows, Gotama is perfect like a star who has "a defined path" to which his disciples like falling leaves follow on. But Kamala and Siddhartha are not like that. They have their own ways and means to follow. Soon they gave up these *Saman* thoughts and "played the game of love, one of the thirty or forty different games which Kamala knew. Her body was as supple as a jagaur and hunter's bow; whoever learned about love from her, learned many pleasures, many secrets. She played with Siddhartha for a long time, repulsed him, overwhelmed him, conquered him, rejoiced at her mastery, until he was overcome and lay exhausted at her side" (Hesse 59). Finally the beautiful courtesan confessed thoughtfully that Siddhartha was the best lover she had had:

> 'You are stronger than others, more supple, more willing. You have learned my art well, Siddhartha. Some day, when I am older, I will have a child by you. And yet, my dear, you have remained a *Saman.* You do not really love me—you love nobody. Is that not true?'
>
> 'May be, said Siddhartha wearily. I am like you. You cannot love either, otherwise how could you practice love as an art? Perhaps people like us cannot love. Ordinary people can—that is their secret' (59).

Often, Siddhartha was caught in a mess when he envied these ordinary people because they had one important thing that he lacked: "the sense of importance with which they had lived their lives, the depth of their pleasures and sorrows, the anxious but sweet happiness of their continual power to love" (62). In riches Siddhartha was lost and discontent of the rich men was reflected in him: "the expressions of discontent, of sickliness, of displeasure, of idleness, of lovelessness. Slowly the soul sickness of rich crept over him" (62). Siddhartha's soul, which had started a new life after parting with Govinda, had been revolved to a standstill; it had been rotten heavy and tired. On the other hand his senses became more active, learned and experienced. He now knew how to transact business, exercise power, amuse women, enjoy rich food, entertain himself in comforts and luxuries. Siddhartha could not notice all these; however, he could notice that "the bright and clear inward voice, that had once awakened in him and had always guided him in his finest hours, had become silent" (63). He had now been lost in wealth, wine and women. Moreover he also "wondered along a strange, twisted path of this last and most base declivity through the game of dice" (63). Through this gambling he derived some passionate pleasure by "squandering of wretched money" (63). One night he was greatly disturbed by a dream in which he visualised how in love play in the pleasure garden Kamala "clasped him to her with extreme fervour, fiercely and tearfully, as if she wanted to once more extract the last sweet drop from this fleeting pleasure. Never had it been so strangely clear to Siddhartha how closely related passion was to death." (64). There he noticed a sad sign in the corners of Kamala's mouth—the fine lines and wrinkles which reminded him "fear of the autumn of life, fear of old age, fear of death. Sighing, he took leave of her, his heart full of misery and secret fear" (65). Again at day break, he also dreamt how the rare bird kept by Kamala in the golden cage was dead and he threw the dead bird and "his heart ached as if he had thrown away with this dead bird all that was good and of value in himself (66). Waking from the dream, Siddhartha was overwhelmed by "a feeling of sadness," and thought that his life had been spent in worthless and senseless manner" (66). He is now "all alone, like a shipwrecked man on the shore" (66).

Gripped by sadness and nausea, Siddhartha reflected the course of his life as the learned *Brahmin* boy, the homeless *Saman,* the Siddhartha with the Buddha, the rich merchant and Kamala's lover. Now the sensual pleasures which he was enjoying have added no vitality to his life and aim: "This whole world of the Kamaswami people had only been a game to him, a dance, a comedy which one watches. Only Kamala was dear to him—had been of value to him,—but was she still? Did he still need her and did she still need him? Were they not playing a game without an end? Was it necessary to live for it? No. This game was called *Sansara,* a game for children, a game which was perhaps enjoyable played once, twice, ten times—but was it worth playing continually?" (67). All these questions stirred Siddhartha. He felt that his game of *Sansara* was finished. Thinking himself as an actor in the drama of life he wants to play a new role in the next scene of the next act of life. Shakespeare's philosophical wise-fool aptly utters in *As You Like It*: "All the world's a stage/ And all the men and women merely players;/ They have their exits and entrances;/ And one man in his time plays many parts;/ His acts being seven ages" (Shakespeare in Tripathy 28). Thus Siddhartha is inspired to play a new different role in the drama of life after serious contemplation and meditation. Throughout the day he reflected about his father, Govinda and Gotama under the mango tree of his pleasure garden. He was rather grieved to note that he left all these intimate and holy people to become a Kamaswami. He, therefore, thought that he must renounce all the riches and possessions and bade good-bye to his pleasure garden in that night when the stars were shining in the sky. Kamaswami searched long, but Siddhartha left his garden not to return. To Kamala, it was natural. She had always thought that Siddhartha was a pilgrim, a *Saman,* without a home. She was happy that she had been able to press Siddhartha "so close to her heart that on that last occasion, had felt so completely possessed and mastered by him" (Hesse 68). Then she opened the golden cage to make the rare song bird fly away and looked at it till the bird disappeared. Thereafter, she never received the visitors and "kept her house closed" (68). However, she was quite happy to learn that "she was with child as a result of her last meeting with Siddhartha" (68).

IV

Siddhartha was gripped by "Death consciousness" in the forest when he had been wandering. Life seemed meaningless, worthless and purposeless anymore. He could not go back to the previous life. Being entangled in *Sansara,* he felt that the life he had lived for many years was past, tasted and drained to a degree of nausea. The songbird was dead; its death, which he had dreamt about, "was the bird in his own heart" (69). He was now full of misery and wished death. Therefore, he wanted some wonders, miracles and misfortunes to fall upon him like being oblivious by wine or death or dying by poison. He wanted the sleep, the greatest sleep by which he would forget everything. Thinking such extreme thoughts, Siddhartha reached the long river "across which a ferryman had once taken him when he was still a young man and had come from Gotama's town" (70). He did not find any meaning to move farther. Even so "why should he go any further, where, and for what purpose?" (70). He rather leaned against the coconut tree in the river bank and looked down into the green water and had a strong desire to be submerged in it. "A chilly emptiness in the water reflected the terrible emptiness in his soul" (70). But, however, when he was indulgent in thinking of losing his "corrupted, rotting body" (70) and his "sluggish and misused soul" (70), suddenly he heard a one syllable word the holy *Om,* the beginning and ending of all *Brahmin* prayers, the meaning of which is the "perfect one" or "perfection." The "slumbering soul" of Siddhartha awakened and he could realise the folly of his action" (71). He could now recognise his urge for suicide, his crime when the *Om* reached his consciousness: "he was conscious of *Brahman,* of the indestructibleness of life" (71). Uttering the *Om,* Siddhartha sank into a deep sleep which was dreamless. After a long refreshing sleep of renewal of life his soul was rejuvenated. Actually he had now a new lease of life, a new birth: "Perhaps he had really died, perhaps he had been drowned and was reborn in another form" (72). But he could not know that he was "Siddhartha self-willed, individualistic. This Siddhartha was somewhat changed, renewed" (72). Waking from the deep and dreamless sleep the refreshed and renewed Siddhartha was much pleased to see Govinda, his childhood friend sitting beside him.

The two friends greeted each other. When Siddhartha asked Govinda about his mission, Govinda replied: "I am not going anywhere. We monks are always on the way, except during the rainy season. We always move from place to place, live according to the rule, preach the gospel, collect alms and then move on. It is always the same. But where are you going Siddhartha?" Siddhartha said "it is the same with me as it is with you, my friend. I am not going anywhere. I am only on the way. I am making a pilgrimage" (74).

Govinda is rather perturbed to note that Siddhartha was making a pilgrimage in "such clothes, in such shoes and with such hair" (74). Siddhartha explains his friend that the world is transitory and everything is subject to change in the flux of time. In the wheel of time Siddhartha, the *Brahmin* and the *Samana* became Siddhartha, the rich man. Again the wheel turned upside down: Siddhartha was no more a rich man. After his friend's departure, Siddhartha felt hungry. The three invincible arts of Siddhartha—fasting, waiting and thinking—his power and strength were no more under his possession. He could no more think. Now he reflects on his situations and conditions: "Things are going backwards with you, he said to himself and laughed, and as he said it, his glance lighted on the river, and he said the river is flowing continually backwards singing merrily. That pleased him immensely; he smiled cheerfully at the river. Was this not the river in which he had once wished to drown himself?" (76).

Siddhartha thought that his life was strange moving along strange paths. From his childhood to manhood Siddhartha travelled a long way experiencing a lot of things and involving himself in many deeds. Now he had been transformed from a man to a child, from a thinker to an ordinary man. "And yet this path has been good and the bird in my breast has not died. But what a path it has been! I have had to experience so much stupidity, so many vices, so much error, so much nausea, disillusionment and sorrow, just in order to become a child again and again anew" (77). He is further reflective and expresses: "I had to experience despair, I had to sink to the greatest mental depths, to thoughts of suicide, in order to experience grace, to hear *Om* again, to sleep deeply again and to awaken refresh again. I had to become a fool again in order to find *Atman* in myself. I had to sin in order to live again. Whither my path yet lead me? This path is stupid, it goes in spirals, perhaps in circles, but whichever way it goes, I will follow it" (77). Siddhartha, therefore, realises that experience is good and real. It makes him true, visionary and wise. As a child he had learnt that materialism and worldly pleasures are worthless and meaningless. But through experience he understood this concept deeper and better. He knew now not through his intellect, "but with my eyes, with my heart, with my stomach" (78). As a *Brahmin* and an ascetic "too much knowledge had hindered him" (79) from understanding the world properly. As a rich man he had indulged in wine, wealth and women and was lost and experienced nausea and despair. Hence "Siddhartha, the pleasure-monger and Siddhartha, the man of property could die. He had died and a new Siddhartha had awakened from his sleep. He also would grow and die. Siddhartha was transitory, all forms were transitory, but today he was young, he was a child—the new Siddhartha—and he was very happy" (79). That is how Siddhartha got new inspiration and new thoughts by looking into the flowing water of the river that had some speciality to tell to the despairing Siddhartha who wanted to drown in the river, of course the old frustrated decayed Siddhartha was drowned and in his place the refreshed Siddhartha "felt a deep love for the flowing water" (80) with new vigour and vitality. Then he thought about the ferryman who took him across this river "from his hut to a new life which is now old and dead. May my present path, my new life, start from there" (81). The newly awakened voice in his heart said to him: "Love this river, stay by it, learn from it" (81). The river gripped Siddhartha's soul. Then Siddhartha went to Vasudeva, the ferryman, a widower who took him across the river again, listened to his "despair and reawakening" and became "compassionate and friendly to him. Both the friends lived in the hut listening to the "voice of the river." Vasudeva taught Siddhartha to learn "the art of listening and Siddhartha learned from it how to listen, to listen with a still heart, with a waiting, open soul, without passion, without desire, without judgement, without opinions" (85).

Siddhartha once asked Vasudeva if he also learned the secret from the river that "there is no such thing as time" (85). Vasudeva assented and explained that the river is everywhere at the same time: "at the source and at the mouth, at the waterfall, at the ferry, at the current, in the ocean and in the mountains, everywhere, and that the present only exists for it, not the shadow of the past, nor the shadow of the future" (86). Siddhartha delightfully told that he learned from the river and it renewed his life: "it was also a river, and Siddhartha the boy, Siddhartha the mature man and Siddhartha the old man were only separated by shadows, not through reality. Siddhartha's previous lives were also not in the past and his death and his return to *Brahma* are not in the future—Nothing was, nothing will be, everything has reality and presence" (86). Both the friends felt that the water of the river "was not just water, but the voice of life, the voice of Being, of perpetual Becoming" (87).

The Buddha, the Illustrious One was going to die. Hearing the news Siddhartha remembered his own "arrogant and precocious words" (88) uttered by him to the great soul and he thought that he was not different from Gotama though he differed from his teachings: "No, a true seeker could not accept any teachings, not if he sincerely wished to find something. But he who had found could give his approval to every path, every goal; nothing separated him from all the other thousands who lived in eclecticity, who breathed the Divine" (88). The news of the approaching death of the Buddha made his followers to be pilgrims for a last *Darshan.* So Kamala, being a follower for a long time after Siddhartha's departure from her had on a pilgrimage to the Buddha along with her eleven-year-old son. The boy got tired on the way. Both mother and son slept and when they were asleep a black snake bit Kamala. The boy cried and as it was near Vasudeva's hut, Vasudeva took her to the hut where she met Siddhartha to be separated from him for ever. She showed him his son and died. "It had been her intention to make a pilgrimage to Gotama, to see the face of Illustrious One, to obtain some of his peace, and instead she had only found him, and it was good, just as good as if she had seen the other" (91). In sorrow, Siddhartha looked "at her dead face" (91) and remembered how in their spring of life "he had compared her lips with a freshly cut fig..." (91). "In this hour he felt more acutely the indestructibleness of every life, the eternity of every moment" (91). Vasudeva prepared some rice but Siddhartha did not take it and listened to the river throughout the night. When the boy was still asleep, "they built a funeral pyre" (92). The boy was deeply sorrow stricken at his mother's death. Though Siddhartha was rather considerate to his son's grief, the "eleven-year-old child was a spoilt mother's boy and had been brought up in the habits of the rich, that he was accustomed to fine food and a soft bed, accustomed to commanding servants" (93). By the passage of time, he felt that his son was "unfriendly and sulky" (94) despite his best effort to make him happy. He was rather "arrogant and defiant" (94) and "showed no respect to the old people" (94). The son brought him sorrow and trouble rather than peace and happiness. However Siddhartha "preferred sorrow and trouble of his love" (94) rather than "happiness and pleasure without the boy" (94).

With the passage of time the boy's obstinacy went on increasing and hence both the old men were in trouble. That is why Vasudeva suggested Siddhartha to send back his son to the town so that the boy would live according to his desires. He would also get education there. But Siddhartha wanted to retain the boy and was rather disturbed to think of the absence of the boy from him. Vasudeva was rather unhappy at the way Siddhartha wished to keep the boy with him to prevent him from committing the errors of making *Sansara.* Vasudeva becomes practical and says: "But if you were to die ten times for him, you would not alter his destiny in the slightest" (96). But Siddhartha had been a little bit indulgent in loving his son:

> It was true that he had never fully lost himself in another person to such an extent as to forget himself; he had never undergone the follies of love for another person. He had never been able to do this, and it had then seemed to him that this was the biggest difference between him and the ordinary people. But now, since his son was there, he, Siddhartha, had become completely like one of the people, through sorrow, through loving. He was madly in love, a fool because of love. Now he also experienced belatedly, for once in his life, the strongest and strangest passion he suffered tremendously through it and yet was uplifted in some way renewed and richer (97).

So the blind passion of love for his son made him forget other aspects of life. It was "a human passion too" (97). This passion was *Sansara.* However this passion was not worthless. It was necessary on part of a human being to experience. "This emotion, this pain, these follies also had to be experienced" (97). One day the son misbehaved his father. He also insulted him by using harsh words. Next day he disappeared not to return again.

Blind with love for his son, he searched and his search was useless. He could not find him and returned in grief from the town.

V

After his long experience, Siddhartha considered "people in a different light." To him now people are "not very clever, not very proud and therefore all the more warm, curious and sympathetic" (102). He considered that the common folk—the businessmen, soldiers and women were his brothers and sisters and did no more consider them to be trivial, absurd and unworthy. Rather he respected these trivial, ordinary common place aspects of life because he could realise "Unity of all life" (103):

> Their vanities, desires and trivialities no longer seemed absurd to him; they had become understandable, lovable and even worthy of respect. There was the blind love of a mother for her child, the blind foolish pride of a fond father for his only son, the blind eager strivings of a young vain woman for ornament and the admiration of men. All these little simple, foolish, but tremendously strong, vital passionate urges and desires no longer seemed trivial to Siddhartha. For their sake he saw people live and do great things, travel, conduct wars, suffer and endure immensely, and he loved them for it. He saw life, vitality, the indestructible and *Brahman* in all their desires and needs. These people were worthy of love and admiration in their blind loyalty, in their blind strength and tenacity.... The men of the world were equal to the thinkers in every other respect and were often superior to them, just as animals in their tenacious undeviating actions in cases of necessity may often seem superior to human beings (103).

This is the real wisdom, Siddhartha experienced in his blood after his life-long search. His knowledge about the world, life and the nature of humanity gradually ripened to take the form of wisdom. His thoughts and contemplations matured slowly through feelings and experiences of a long, long search,—the real worthy search about life. He could attain the "harmony, the knowledge of the eternal perfection of the world, and unity" (103) which he had seen in Vasudeva's old childlike face long since he had met him: "Within Siddhartha there slowly grew and ripened the knowledge of what wisdom really was and the goal of his long seeking. It was nothing but a preparation of the soul, a capacity, a secret art of thinking, feeling and breathing thoughts of unity at every moment of life" (103).

However, Siddhartha was still lavishly hurt to see his son. He was "consumed by longing" (104) to see him and could listen to the sound of the river:

> The river flowed softly and gently; it was in the dry season but its voice rang out strangely. It was laughing, it was distinctly laughing! The river was laughing clearly and merrily at the old ferryman. Siddhartha stood still; he bent over the water in order to hear better. He saw his face reflected in the quietly moving water, and there was something in this reflection and that reminded him of something he had forgotten, and when he reflected on it he remembered (104).

This nostalgic reiteration is a very significant aspect in everybody's life. This is the whole truth about human life. Man, not only knows this, he also feels it. And this feeling is the real wisdom. By traversing throughout his life, Siddhartha could now realise the Basic Truth at the fag end of his journey of search:

> His face resembled that of another person, whom he had once known and loved and even feared. It resembled the face of his father, the *Brahmin.* He remembered how once, as a youth, he had compelled his father to let him go and join the ascetics, how he had taken leave of him, how he had gone and never returned. Had not his father died long ago, alone, without having seen his son again? Did he not expect the same fate? Was it not a comedy, a strange and a stupid thing, this repetition, this course of events in a fateful circle ? (104)

The internal conflict of Siddhartha trembles the whole of his body, mind and spirit. He wants to escape suffering, which is simply impossible. The repetition of suffering is a continuous process in this immanent universe. Nobody can challenge the doings of an immanent fate. However Siddhartha, influenced by illusions and without conquering them, continued to suffer by challenging the power of fate: "The wound still smarted; he still rebelled against his fate. There was still no serenity and conquest of his suffering" (104). However after returning to the hut he confesses the whole Truth to Vasudeva because of the "unconquerable desire to confess" (104) in him: his "smarting wound" and going to the town in search of his son, being envious to see happy fathers, "his knowledge of the folly of such things, the laughing of the river at him and so on. Vasudeva listens the whole thing like a "motionless listener"(105) "absorbing his confession as a tree absorbs the rain" (105). "Vasudeva felt his troubles, his anxieties and his secret hopes flow across to him and then return again" (105). He is a very patient listener who knows the "art of listening" (104). Gradually Siddhartha like Arjuna of *The Mahabharat* realises that "this motionless man was the river itself, that He was God Himself, that he was eternity itself" (105). He is a *stitaprajna* like Sri Krishna the *Nirbikara* soul, the immovable spirit, the man who has attained wisdom, who listens the entire thing and directs "his somewhat weakened glance at him" (106): "He did not speak, but his face silently radiated love and serenity, understanding and knowledge." Then he leads him to the river bank and tells him to listen to the river deeper and better with due attention:

> 'You have heard it laugh,' he said, 'but you have not heard every thing. Let us listen; you will hear more.' They listened. The many-voiced song of the river echoed softly. Siddhartha looked into the river and saw many pictures in the flowing water. He saw his father, lonely, mourning for his son; he saw himself, lonely, also with the bonds of longing for his faraway son; he saw his son, also lonely, the boy eagerly advancing along the burning path of life's desires, each one concentrating on his goal, each one obsessed by his goal, each one suffering. The river's voice was sorrowful. It sang with yearning and sadness, flowing towards its goal. 'Do you hear?' asked Vasudeva's mute glance. Siddhartha nodded. 'Listen better' whispered Vasudeva (106).

Siddhartha could listen better, deeper and more patiently and could realise the "music of life" (107). The goal of everybody—his father, his own life, his son, Kamala, Govinda—is "yearning, desiring, suffering" (106). The music of life is there in the voice of the river: "The river's voice is full of longing, full of smarting woe, full of insatiable desire" (106). In "Dover Beach," Arnold compares religious faith to an ocean and talks how Sophocles had a similar experience of listening to the sound of the ocean waves and he too found the note of sadness in that sound. That sound reminded him of all the wild confusions and distresses that prevail in human life. Once there was perfect faith in the world. The sea of faith had enclosed the entire world. Since the world is losing faith and becoming sceptic in its outlook with all its doubts and disbeliefs, there is only misery left. As Arnold notes his own sadness in the sounds of the sea waves so also Siddhartha observes his life's rhythm in the ripples of the river (Tripathy 37). After the death of Abhimanyu, Arjun's despair/ disillusion was removed only when he was taken to *swarga* (Heaven) and Abhimanyu disowned him as his father. These mythical references are just visionary glimpses that enlighten as to visualise truth and wisdom. All his relations have the same objective of reaching the goal:

> All the waves and water hastened, suffering, towards goals, many goals, to the waterfall, to the sea, to the current, to the ocean and all goals were reached and each one was succeeded by another. The water changed to vapour and rose, became rain and came down again, became spring, brook and river, changed anew, flowed anew. But the yearning voice altered. It still echoed sorrowfully, searchingly, but other voices accompanied it, voices, laughing and lamenting voices, hundreds of voices, thousands of voices (Hesse 106-107).

He had, of course, listened to all these voices much before. However, they "sounded somewhat different today. He does not find any distinction among the different voices": the merry voice from the weeping voice, the childish voice from the manly voice (107). The lamenting voice of sorrow stricken people, "the laughter of the wise, the cry of indignation and groan of the dying" (107) are all "interwoven and interlocked, entwined in a thousand ways" (107). The world constitutes all of them—the voices, the goals, the yearnings, the sorrows; the pleasures, the good and the evil. This stream of events together constitutes the music of life. In the process he is not absorbed in one of these voices. He is rather detached from all of them. That makes him wise like Arjuna of *The Mahabharat.* Arjuna attains wisdom and understands the meaning of "detachment" and "unity of being" after he sees the *Viswarupa* in Sri Krishan's Soul as Siddhartha experiences the vision of "unity of being" in the river. In *Adhyaya* XI (*slokas* 9, 12, 13, 15-18, 38-40, 43, 44), Arjuna sees God as the "all embracing universal spirit before which the pairs of opposites of good and evil, pleasure and pain, light and darkness, and the like disappear" (Rajagopalachari 113). It has been said that Arjuna was given the divine eye to have the Vision of the universal and "the trans-dichotomous *Viswarupa* which transcends the Relative and the Partial" (113). That means Arjuna's soul catches "a glimpse of God, the universal Immanent Being, when by a pure and dedicated life, and by the practice of serenity and constant meditation, the *Yogi* succeeds in merging his Self in the universe and realises the ultimate oneness of all existence" (113). Thus Siddhartha's soul attains peace, perfection, "the *Om*." Now his Self had merged into unity (Hesse 108). All conflicts now vanish from his mind; he attains wisdom and his Self is merged with the stream of life: "There shone in his face the serenity of knowledge, of one who is no longer confronted with conflict of desires, who has found salvation, who is in harmony with the stream of events, with the stream of life, full of sympathy and compassion, surrendering himself to the stream, belonging to the unity of all things" (108).

Siddhartha gets his *sidhi*; he attains *Nirvana.* Vasudeva feels that his work is over by seeing "the serenity of knowledge shining" (108) in Siddhartha's eyes. He bids farewell to the hut, the river and Siddhartha. Now Siddhartha watches Vasudeva with "great joy and gravity" (108) and sees "his steps full of peace, his face glowing, his form full of light" (108).

VI

"Seeking" is a continuous process. It is not to end. Seeking should be the way of life's journey. This is the conviction of Govinda, Siddhartha's friend. Towards the end of the novel, he comes to Siddhartha for a dialogue on philosophical doctrines and thoughts. Though Govinda "had lived his life according to the rule" (109) he was still "restless in his heart and his seeking was unsatisfied" (109). Meeting Siddhartha, Govinda says: "I am indeed old...but I have never ceased seeking. I will never cease seeking. That seems to be my destiny. It seems to me that you also have sought. Will you talk to me a little about it my friend?" Siddhartha said: "What could I say to you that would be of value, except that perhaps you seek too much, that as a result of your seeking you cannot find" (109-10).

From experience Siddhartha realises that a person who goes on seeking and seeking, is unable to find or absorb or assimilate many things. It is because of the fact that "seeking" makes the seeker goal-oriented and unreceptive. On the other hand "finding" means "to be free, to be receptive, to have no goal" (110). A seeker is inclined to achieve his goal and in the process of seeking he is unable to "see many things that are under your nose" (110). Govinda is rather disillusioned and before he takes goodbye from Siddhartha he asks: "Have you a doctrine, belief or knowledge which you uphold, which helps you to live and do right?" (111). To this query, Siddhartha responds cooly and utters that he distrusts doctrines and teachers though he has many teachers by now: a beautiful courtesan, a rich merchant and a dice player, one of the Buddha's wandering monks and so on. He has learned something from each of them, and hence obliged to all of them. But his learning comes from this river and Vasudeva, the predecessor ferryman: "But most of all, I have learned from this river and from my predecessor, Vasudeva. He was a simple man; he was not a thinker but he realised the essential as well as Gotama. He was a holy man, a saint." But Govinda is not to believe that Siddhartha has any teachers. He has the conviction that Siddhartha has some knowledge by which he lives. Siddhartha agrees that he has some occasional knowledge and certain thoughts. But he has been greatly impressed by one thought that is: "Wisdom is not communicable. The wisdom which a wise man tries to communicate always sounds foolish" (111-12). Siddhartha goes on pleading that he has discovered that "knowledge can be communicated, but not wisdom...one can find it, be fortified by it, do wonders through it, but one cannot communicate and teach it" (112). He also feels that "in every truth the opposite is equally true" (112):

> Everything that is thought and expressed in words is one-sided, only half the truth; it all lacks totality, completeness, unity when the Illustrious Buddha thought about the world, he had to divide it into *Sansara* and *Nirvana,* into illusion and truth, into suffering and salvation. One cannot do otherwise, there is no other method for those who teach. But the world itself, being in and around us, is never one-sided. Never is a man or a deed wholly *Sansara* or wholly *Nirvana*; never is a man wholly a saint or a sinner. This only seems so because we suffer the illusion that time is something real. Time is not real, Govinda. I have realised this repeatedly. And if time is not real, that the dividing line that seems to lie between this world and eternity, between suffering and bliss, between good and evil, is also an illusion (112).

This truth puzzles Govinda as Arjuna is puzzled by Sri Krishna's discourses to him before the *Mahabharat* war (*Bhagavad Gita*). It also reminds me of the puzzle of Ursula when Birkin discusses with her about this world and life (D.H. Lawrence: *Women in Love*). It is very difficult to comprehend the Truth, attained through realisation and experience. It cannot be taught to a person. The disciple is to experience the wisdom in his blood, in his heart and in his mind. Otherwise, the Truth will remain an enigma to him. That has happened to Govinda and hence he wants to listen more about this thought from Siddhartha, the realiser, the experiencer and the discoverer of the whole Truth, the only Truth: "Listen, my friend! I am a sinner and you are a sinner, but some day the sinner will be a *Brahma* again, will some day attain *Nirvana,* will some day become a Buddha. But this "some day" is illusion; it is only a comparison. The sinner is not on the way to a Buddha-like state; he is not evolving, although our thinking cannot conceive things otherwise" (112).

According to Siddhartha, there is no such thing as the imperfect world is evolving towards perfection. At every moment the world is perfect; all sinners are holy. Every child is a potential old man. Everybody has death in him. Every sin has certain grace, purity: "the Buddha exists in the robber and dice player; the robber exists in the *Brahmin*" (113). Time is unifying: there is simultaneousness in the past, present and future. T.S. Eliot in *Four Quartets* has rightly remarked: "Time past and time future/ what might have been and what has been/ Point to one end, which is always present (14). In this world everything is good: "...death as well as life, sin as well as holiness, wisdom as well as folly." Failure is as important as success because failure is the pillar of success:

> Everything is necessary, everything needs only my agreement, my assent, my loving understanding; then all is well with me and nothing can harm me. I learned through my body and soul that it was necessary for me to sin, that I needed lust, that I had to strive for property and experience nausea and the depths of despair in order to learn to love the world, and no longer compare it with some kind of desired imaginary world, some imaginary vision of perfection, but to leave it as it is, to love it and be glad to belong to it (Hesse 113).

Everything has some value and meaning. Nothing is unnecessary, insignificant. In the scheme of creation even a stone is of paramount importance. Each stone is "*Om* in its own way; each one is *Brahma*" (114). Things are more important than words because they are real; they are true. One should love "things" rather than "words." That is why Siddhartha considers "teachings" as useless because "they have no hardness, no softness, no colours, no corners, no smell, no taste—they have nothing but words" (114). As such teachings can never give us peace. There are many words for "salvation and virtue," "*Sansara* and *Nirvana.*" "*Nirvana* is not a thing; there is only the word *Nirvana*" (114). But Govinda argues that *Nirvana* is not only a word, "it is also a thought" (114). However Siddhartha pleads that things are the only Truth about this world:

> It may be a thought, but I must confess, my friend, that I do not differentiate very much between thoughts and words. Quite frankly, I do not attach great importance to thoughts either. I attach more importance to things. For example, there was a man at this ferry who was my predecessor and teacher. He was a holy man who for many years believed only in the river and nothing else. He noticed that the river's voice spoke to him. He learned from it; it educated and taught him. The river seemed like a God and for many years he did not know that every wind, every cloud, every bird, every beetle is equally divine and knows and can teach just as well as the esteemed river. But when this holy man went off into the woods, he knew everything; he knew more than you and I, without teachers, without books, just because he believed in the river (115).

Govinda is not rather convinced by these strange thoughts of Siddhartha because in this world all these things—stone, tree, river—are unreal, "the illusion of *Maya*, only image and appearance" (115). Siddhartha is not at all bothered even if all the things of the world are illusory, *Maya*, because he himself would also be an illusion and fit into the entire scheme of the illusory world. The only doctrine he believes is that "love is the most important thing in the world" (115): "It may be important to great thinkers to examine the world, to explain and despise it. But I think it is only important to love the world, not to despise it, not for us to hate each other, but to be able to regard the world and ourselves and all beings with love, admiration and respect" (116). This concept of love is reinforced when we read the novel, *Women in Love* by D.H. Lawrence where Lawrence emphasises the human relationship based on man-man love, man-woman love and man-cosmos relationship (541 and 169-70).

Even in *A Passage to India,* Forster emphasises the concept of love and relationship among all beings for smooth running of the universe. However Govinda is not yet convinced. He rather argues that the "Illustrious One" called love as illusion. On the contrary he taught "benevolence, forbearance, sympathy, patience—but not love. He forbade us to bind ourselves to earthly love" (115-16). But Siddhartha dismisses this because Govinda's understanding is confused, not clear. He argues that his "conviction of love" is in apparent contradiction to the "teachings of Gotama." In actuality, there is no contradiction. It is rather "the conflict of words" "the maze of meanings" (116). This apparent contradiction is an illusion. This great teacher, Gotama, had never hated humanity. He had tremendous affinity to and love for this mankind. That is why he sacrificed the whole of his life in teaching people and thinking about their welfare: "His deeds and life are more important to me than his opinions. Not in speech or thought do I regard him as a great man, but in his deeds and life" (116). These "strange thoughts" of Siddhartha stirred the mind and heart of Govinda. They reminded him of Gotama's doctrines which "are clear, straightforward, comprehensible" (116). On the other hand, Siddhartha's ideas seem crazy, strange, wild and laughable. Despite this he has high esteem for Siddhartha: "His ideas may be strange, his words may sound foolish, but his glance and his hand, his skin and his hair all radiate a purity, peace, serenity, gentleness and saintliness which I have never seen in any man since the recent death of our Illustrious teacher" (116-17). Then Govinda kisses the forehead of smiling Siddhartha "compelled by a great love and presentiment to obey him" (117). This action changed the whole conviction of Govinda. He had a vision of the Truth; he experienced the wisdom in his blood. In his vision he could see thousands of forms in their interrelationship, interdestructiveness and renewal of the whole thing:

> He saw all these forms and faces in a thousand relationships to each other, loving, hating and destroying each other and become newly born. Each one was mortal, a passion, painful example of all that is transitory. Yet none of them died, they only changed, were always reborn, continually had a new face; only time stood between one face and another. And all these forms and

> faces rested, flowed, reproduced, swam past and merged into each other, and over them all there was continually something thin glass or ice, like a transparent skin, shell, form or mask of water—and this mask was Siddhartha's smiling face which Govinda touched with his lips at that moment. And Govinda saw that this mask-like smile, this smile of unity over the flowing forms, this smile of simultaneousness over the thousands of births and deaths—this smile of Siddhartha—was exactly the same as the calm, delicate, impenetrable, perhaps gracious, perhaps mocking, wise, thousand-fold smile of Gotama, the Buddha, as he had perceived it with awe a hundred times. It was in such a manner, thus Govinda knew, that the perfect one smiled (118).

Govinda is "overwhelmed by a feeling of great love" for Siddhartha. "He bowed low, right down to the ground in front of the man sitting there motionless whose smile reminded him of everything that he had ever loved in his life, of everything that had ever been of value and holy in his life" (119). So love and relationship are most important in this world. All other things are transitory, brittle. Man must learn to live through love and interrelationship. He must renounce hatred. He must not despise because there is not much distinction between good and evil, sin and unholiness.

VII

Life is really an enigma, a mystery, a puzzle. It is difficult on the part of a man to understand life through theories, teachings and abstract conceptualisations. No doubt, these are very important to give a systematic shape to our understanding. But all of them will be just empty cries in the wilderness if they are not founded on a strong base of experience and realisation. Through experience and realisation, our convictions, conceptualisation and understanding become strong and deep-rooted. Knowledge has no meaning till it is transformed into wisdom in our blood and flesh, mind and soul. Knowing is not as important as realisation and understanding. It is, therefore, Siddhartha, the learned *Brahmin* disciple of a high standing loses himself in the wilderness and finds no direction from his knowledge from theoretically high doctrines, great scriptures and the best teachings of Gotama. He lacks experience about the world, about life, about the needs of "his own Self." How can he attain *Nirvana* or *Atman,* through "self denial" and hatred to this "strange, beautiful and wonderful great world." Knowledge and experience must mingle to fuse together to be one, to be transformed into wisdom. That is why Siddhartha's pilgrimage is certainly a wonderfully real life's journey to attain peace and salvation through the real understanding and wisdom about the world. In Mulk Raj Anand's most recent novel *Nine Moods of Bharata* (1998), the protagonist, Azad understands the suffering of the Indian masses under the British Raj through his pilgrimage to Ajanta caves. He regards his pilgrimage to the caves as the "pilgrimage of pain" (Anand 165). The Buddha had advised his disciples to wander if they really wanted to understand the world properly: "Go you oh *Bhikshus* wander for love of many! For welfare of many! Out of compassion for many—who are suffering" (169). Even Vivekananda has emphasised the practice rather than theory of all concepts: "Even if you have a burning thirst for God, or have gained the Guru, unless you have along with it the *Abhyasa,* unless you practice what you have been taught, you cannot get realisation. When all these are firmly established in you, then you will reach the goal" (408). He further tells us that we must "go beyond this *Sansara*—not only to renounce the world, but to give up heaven too; ay, not only to give up evil, but to give up good too; and thus go beyond all, beyond all this phenomenal real existence,—the Absolute, Existence—knowledge—Bliss, which is *Brahman*" (409).

It is, of course, not proper to dismiss that Siddhartha as a great learned *Brahmin* disciple, as hard-striving ascetic and as a rich indulgent *Sansari,* is of no use and worth in his final life as a great saint and wise man. Travelling through all these inevitably necessary tracks, Siddhartha's understanding becomes firm, considerable, true and deep about the world and life. Finally he has attained calmness; he has become a detached soul, a *stitaprajna.* His whole life's pilgrimage has become a continuous process from being to becoming, still becoming, still attaining, still learning, still assimilating—all learning into a "unity of being and becoming." Wisdom includes everything; it is eternal. It is based on interrelationships, interconnections, interactions and continuity. It is coherent bringing all cohesive forces together. It is, therefore, Siddhartha's pilgrimage is an enduring attractive concept which inspires us to be individualistic and unique through our own experiences to make ourselves truly wise and attain peace and calmness.

WORKS CITED

Anand, Mulk Raj. *Nine Moods of Bharata* (New Delhi: Arnold Associates, 1998).

Arnold, Matthew. "Dover Beach," *Joys of Poetry* 1986. Ed. Biyotkesh Tripathy (New Delhi: S. Chand & Company Ltd., 1991) 37.

Bacon, Francis. "Of Travel" *English Essayists* (Delhi/ Bombay/ Madras: OUP, 1995) 11.

Belloc, Hilaire. "The Idea of a Pilgrimage" *English Essayists* (1987; Delhi: OUP, 1995) 112.

Eliot, T.S. *Four Quartets* (1944; rpt. Delhi: OUP, 1980).

——. "Journey of the Magi" *Joys of Poetry.* Ed. Biyotkesh Tripathy (1986; New Delhi. S. Chand & Company Ltd., 1991) 92.

Forster, E.M. *A Passage to India,* (1924; New York: Penguin, 1982).

Hesse, Hermann. *Siddhartha.* Trans. Hilda Rosner. (1922; 1960; Delhi: Rupa & Co., 1992).

Hick, John H. *Philosophy of Religion* (3rd ed. 1983; New Delhi: Prentice Hall of India Private Limited, 1987).

Hussain, S. Abid. *The National Culture of India* (1956; New Delhi: National Book Trust, 1978).

Lawrence, D.H. *Women in Love* (1921; 1960; rpt. Harmondsworth: Penguin 1981).

Rajagopalachari, C. *Bhagavad Gita* (1963; Bombay: Bharatiya Vidya Bhavan, 1991).

——. *Mahabharata* (1951; Bombay: Bharatiya Vidya Bhavan, 1990).

Shakespeare, William. "All the World's a Stage" *Joys of Poetry* ed. Biyotkesh Tripathy (1986; New Delhi: S. Chand & Company Ltd., 1991) 28.

Sinha, Susant K. (ed.), *English Essayists* (1986; 1987; Delhi: OUP, 1995).

Srinivasan, R. *Facets of Indian Culture* (1962; Bombay: Bharatiya Vidya Bhavan, 1980).

Subramaniyan, N.S. *The Bhagawad Gita* (1980; rpt. New Delhi: Tarang Paperbacks) (Vikas Publishing House Pvt. Ltd., 1993).

Vireswarananda, Swami. Trans. *Srimad Bhagavad Gita* (Madras: Sri Rama Krishna Math, 1983).

Vivekananda, Swami. *Lectures from Colombo to Almora* (Calcutta: Advaita Ashrama, 1990).

8

Self-Delineation in Fiction: A Comparative Study of Select Works of Nayantara Sahgal and Akilon

RANJIT SINGH

SEVERAL PREDOMINANT autobiographical elements can be perceived in the novels of the North Indian English writer Nayantara Sahgal and the Tamil writer Akilon. These are, by and large, the impressive characters and incidents in the lives of the authors that have found their way into their world of imaginative writing. Through extraordinary craftsmanship and characteristic vision the novelists have succeeded in transforming highly personal materials into artistic entities. Nayantara Sahgal makes no bones of the above fact:

> Everything around the writer is material for a novel.... All one's material comes from real life.... One generally draws on one's own experience or someone else's experience (qtd. in John 13).

Akilon, too readily acknowledges the close link between a writer's life and his craft in his autobiography *Eluttum Vālkkaiyum* (Letters and Life):

> There is a very intimate relationship between a writer's private life and his writing. The experiences of his personal life constitute the very seed of his creation and serve as sustenance and support for his growth as a writer (9).

While the mazy bond connecting a novelist's life and his world of fiction is complex and difficult to analyse or unravel, quite often the autobiographies of writers offer unambiguous clues with regard to the closeness between a writer and his/her work. Sahgal's two autobiographies—*Prison and Chocolate Cake* (1954) and *From Fear Set Free* (1962)—provide a valuable source for a proper appreciation of the novelist and her works. Both of Sahgal's autobiographies present intertwined strains of the personal as well as national issues. She records her experiences of childhood and adolescence, which stand out in her memory, in her first autobiography entitled *Prison and Chocolate Cake*. Sahgal's second autobiography *From Fear Set Free* deals with the mature years of her life. Further, Sahgal's recent publication, a collection of letters entitled *Relationship: Extracts from a Correspondence* (1994), by Nayantara Sahgal and E.N. Mangat Rai gives additional intimate glimpses into her marital problems which are echoed in several contexts of her fiction. Akilon's autobiography *Eluttum Vālkkaiyum* (1978) where he gives an account of his own life from the year of his birth 1922 to 1965, helps us recognise some of the subtle autobiographical overtones in his novels. As Akilon himself puts it, the book helps us "not only to know something of my own (Akilon's) life story but also the story of my stories" (*Eluttum Vālkkaiyum* 4).

Autobiographical details with regard to Sahgal and Akilon can be gleaned from the works like *A Time to Be Happy*, *Storm in Chandigarh*, *The Day in Shadow, A Situation in New Delhi* and *Rich Like Us* of Sahgal and *Peṇ* (The Woman), *Inpa Ninaivu* (The Happy Recall), *Putu Veḷḷam* (The New Flood), *Pāvai Viḷakku* (The Maiden Lamp) and *Koḷḷaikkāran* (The Bandit) of Akilon. Of these novels, *The Day in Shadow* of Sahgal and *Koḷḷaikkāran* and *Pāvai Viḷakku* of Akilon present the lives of protagonists who bear striking resemblances to their own creators and their sensibilities reflect a remarkable similitude to the minds which fashioned them.

As regards Sahgal, the autobiographical elements are uppermost in her novel *The Day in Shadow*. Simrit, the protagonist in this gyno-centric novel bears in many respects the image of her author. The novel presents the struggle of a young, courageous and well-endowed modern Indian woman beset with the unfair and gruesome conditions of divorce settlement handed out to her by a cruel, vulgar, male dominated and chauvinistic world. The agony of Simrit as a divorcee seems to find some authentic echoes from Sahgal's personal life as it was written in 1970 soon after Sahgal's own divorce in 1967. Sahgal herself acknowledges the above fact in her article "Of Divorce and Hindu Woman." Referring to *The Day in Shadow* she observes with utmost candour:

> In this book I tried to figure out something that has happened to me—the shattering experience of divorce. I wanted to show how even in a free country like ours, where women are equal citizens, a woman can be criminally exploited without creating a ripple (12 Dec. 1971).

Like her creator, Simrit is a free-lance journalist and writer who gets married to a businessman of her own choice and experiences a sense of bewilderment and a shattering emotional shock of her divorce and the brutal consequences of an unfair divorce settlement, inflicted on her after seventeen long years of married life. Even to start with, Simrit marries outside her caste and hence her choice is not welcomed by her parents: "Her Brahmin parents with their instinctive withdrawal from anything outside the fold had been frankly upset at her choice of a businessman husband" (3). This is almost an exact reflection of what Sahgal herself feels about her personal choice of a life partner outside her fold:

> Had my marriage been arranged I should not have married Gautam. We should in that case, have married partners from our own province and caste, eliminating at the outset as many seeds of potential conflict as are humanly possible to foresee (*From Fear Set Free* 32).

Just like Sahgal, Simrit too is overburdened with heavy taxes because of the divorce settlement. In fact, at one stage, Sahgal felt so overwhelmed with the enormity of her tax burden that she eventually overcame her problem of tax only through her own independent efforts. In her interview to Jasbir Jain, she says:

> My husband defrauded me also. Not only defrauded me but hung me with taxes I would not have had otherwise. I had a huge struggle after the divorce to make money and I made it. I feel pleased that I managed to do it, not by any inheritance or any such thing but by my own efforts (185).

In the novel, Simrit experiences an enormous burden at the imposition of tax on her. And all she experiences within is a loathsome sense of self-pity and she calls herself "an overloaded donkey…with its back breaking" (56). She pleads with her husband Som's lawyer Moolchand that she does not need any share left in her name as all shares mean to her only taxes: "But I don't want shares left in my name. As long as they are, I'll have to pay this crippling tax and whatever I earn will just be wiped out by the tax, don't you see?" (56).

After her divorce, Sahgal seems to have gained a certain degree of conventional wisdom which suggests to her the fact that marriage ties are indissoluble:

> A long relationship like marriage has for years sent out too many shoots and tentacles. Its holds spread out and go deep down. You can cut off the part of the plant that shows, but the undergrowth persists. The pattern of marriage is ineradicable.… I don't think the extent of this struck me until I saw Gautam again and thought, "Here am I planning to live with another man where there is this unfinished business between this man and me" (*Relationship* 197).

Sahgal reiterates this view again in the same novel while describing Simrit's feelings after her divorce: "The tissues of marriage could be dissolved by human act but its anatomy went on and on" (64); "In some inescapable way part of her would be always married to Som" (220).

In real life, Nayantara Sahgal after having been separated from and abandoned by her husband, found a true companion in a Christian Government official, E.N. Mangat Rai, I.C.S. and got married to him. In *The Day in Shadow* she makes her protagonist Simrit too find comfort and comradeship in the company of a Christian Member of Parliament, Raj Garg, whom she marries in the end. Just like the novelist, Simrit, a divorcee, has her own important responsibility of looking after her children. Thus, the autobiographical tone is more predominant in this novel than in any other of the Sahgal canon.

With regard to Akilon, "Life and literature are inseparable.... Life influences the artist writer and in its turn writing creates life. Life itself offers him the bedrock of thematic elements" (*Eluttum Vālkkaiyum* 10). Hence, Akilon fictionalised several of his life experiences into short stories and novels. His novel *Koḷḷaikkāran* is perhaps his most autobiographical work in presenting certain strange but authentic experiences of a ten-year old village boy who happens to run into a bandit of the Village Thekkatoor. In the introduction to the above work Akilon writes:

> Can we have a peep into the life struggles, values, fluctuations of social status and habits in vogue in the rural life of those times? In a way, this may be called a little historical account of my father's days (5-6).

In this work Akilon uses the first person narrative in order to present his version of history of a bygone age with a rare sureness of touch. This novella is thus a self acknowledged recollection of Akilon's past especially an account of the dominant bandits of the times who came eventually under the custody of his father, a village officer in Thekkatoor. In *Eluttum Vālkkaiyum*, Akilon recalls some of the moments which he savours even now as adult:

> For a few months I would be the pet of the convicted thieves. They would tell me their experiences.... Those who read my novella *Koḷḷaikkāran* may be able to see in it the Thekkatoor of my childhood, its bandits, my parents and myself (43-44).

The narrator who is very close to Thangaswamy, a bandit, is at times even borne on his shoulders into the forest, receiving delicious dates, wild fruits and similar other exhilarating gifts.

Perhaps the most predominantly autobiographical among Akilon's works, is his celebrated novel *Pāvai Viḷakku* which dwells on several of Akilon's personal experiences as a writer, presented through the portrayal of Tanikacalam, the protagonist. Discussing *Pāvai Viḷakku* as an autobiographical novel, M. Ramalingam, a friend of Akilon, makes the following comment in his *Akilonin Kalaiyum Karuttum* (Akilon's Art and Poetics):

> Akilon opens his novel with an introduction saying 'the person whose story I am going to write here is a close friend of mine. However, as we have been moving very close with each other over so many years, he himself has revealed to me many facts about his personal life.' Akilon does not present his story in the first person narrative but by using the third person narrative he has concealed his personal history to a considerable extent beyond any possibility of recognition. Isn't it quite possible that the so-called 'close friend' he mentions, may be none other than Akilon himself? (53-54).

Akilon himself acknowledges *Pāvai Viḷakku* as autobiographical in his *Kataik Kalai* (The Art of Story Telling):

> *Pāvai Viḷakku* is considered by many as a very important novel among my works of the middle phase. To some extent, this novel is based on the internal and external struggles of my life.... I believe the real reason for the enormous success of this novel has been 'the expression of experience and emotional truth' (95).

Just like Akilon in his personal life, Tanikacalam too has to face many a challenge, like unemployment and poverty. As a writer Tanikacalam proves himself utterly fearless and honest just as Akilon himself aspired to be. Akilon was persuaded by his mother and grandmother to marry his uncle's daughter Patammal. In the novel this important incident is fictionalised in the scene where Tanikacalam is strongly urged to marry Gauri, his uncle's daughter an orthodox village girl. Again, Uma of *Pāvai Viḷakku* has her parallel in Swarnalatha, a teacher in Trichy and an ardent admirer of Akilon who even dared to resign her job in order to co-habit with Akilon and his wife in Madras, much in the same manner as Uma does in the novel. In his autobiography Akilon observes:

> Towards the close of *Pāvai Viḷakku* Uma breathes her last. But during that time in my personal life the other woman (Swarnalatha) who could not bear the strain of emotional struggle was fighting for her own life (312).

We can easily see Akilon has fictionalised some of the events of his personal life in his work *Pāvai Viḷakku* that was being serialised during the time in *Kalki*, a popular Tamil weekly. Akilon himself makes a clear breast of the fact that several incidents described in his *Pāvai Viḷakku* had been contemporaneous events of his personal life:

> Various episodes and emotional conflicts depicted in *Pāvai Viḷakku* were nothing but actual experiences happening in my own personal life. I was recording the experiences of my private world simply in those episodes of my novel, gilding the real life events with an imaginative touch (*Eluttum Vālkkaiyum* 310).

One such event depicted in the novel is, while Akilon was writing his serial novel *Nencin Alaikaḷ* (The Waves of the Heart) in *Kalai Makal*õ he fell ill with high fever and was strictly advised by the doctors to take rest but he carried on with his writing and contributed his monthly instalment of the novel by dictating the rest of the episodes to his wife from bed. This incident finds a place in *Pāvai Viḷakku* in two episodes. Once, Tanikacalam cannot write on account of high fever, and later on when he ends up with a fracture in his arm, Uma writes down the story for him with Tanikacalam dictating to her from bed. Akilon himself refers to this incident in the *Katai Kali*. "Just as Tanikacalam in *Pāvai Viḷakku* makes Uma write down the story as he dictates; I too dictated the story to my wife who wrote it down for me" (78).

Yet another incident which eventually left Akilon emotionally upset was the death of his two-year old beloved daughter Amirthavalli, stung by a scorpion, an incident Akilon records in a moving passage in his autobiography: "My child took a rebirth as Tanikacalam's girl child 'Kalyani' in *Pāvai*

Viḷakku" (301). In the novel, Kalyani a toddler falls down from the stair-case as she steps down, unnoticed by her mother and grandmother who are busy in the kitchen and later dies despite all the medical care given as did Amirthavalli. It is interesting to note that Akilon's child Amirthavalli was named after his mother Amirthammal and Tanikacalam's child Kalyani is named after his mother Kalyaniammal. There are also some other similitudes between Tanikacalam, a Gandhian, who turns down bribe and throws himself into the freedom struggle playing an active role in the August Revolt of 1942 and Akilon himself. Thus certain unmistakable associations can be perceived between Akilon and Tanikacalam.

Thus the worlds depicted in the works of Sahgal and Akilon are not totally divorced from the one which groomed their personalities in youth. It is also equally true that their imaginative creations are not totally identical with the lives and events connected with the actual experiences of their writers. A considerable part of certain episodes which have made an indelible impression on them have been imaginatively redesigned in their fiction. Undoubtedly, the episodes and the events culled out of their memories not only lend colour to their worlds of fiction but also an unmistakable touch of realism and authenticity. Discussing the fundamental issues of "Thematology" Weisstein approvingly quotes from Curtius:

> The meaning of literary work results from the poet's personal experience which forms a kind of basic pattern for which he seeks a corresponding subject during the creative process (126).

True to this statement, Sahgal and Akilon have also exploited their own personal experiences as basic patterns of their creative works.

The bitter and painful experiences of Nayantara Sahgal as divorcee have been projected through Simrit in *The Day in Shadow* which is presented from sociological rather than personal perspective. The novelist's private experiences are analysed in the novel in the context of the social forces she had to encounter in life. In the novel, focus soon shifts from the portrait of an individual to the depiction of a struggle that depicts simply the attempt of an Indian woman who is bent on liberating herself from the oppressive forces of a male-oriented and male-dominated society. The discussion of the issue relating to single women in Indian society provides the novelist with an ample scope for depicting the subjection and exploitation of women in a society dominated by male chauvinists.

Akilon's autobiographical novels *Koḷḷaikkāran and Pāvai Viḷakku* on the other hand, being more intensely and subjectively autobiographical, present details from the author's own life, in critical retrospection. Several ups and downs including a variety of moments of agony and ecstasy from the personal world of Akilon, can be directly perceived from his works. A considerable part of his personal life tracing his growth and development from boyhood to manhood is depicted with exceptional vividness and authenticity through the lives of his protagonists in these novels.

With regard to Sahgal, the focus on the artist's life in *The Day in Shadow* covers only a limited range of her life, namely that of a hapless divorcee, struggling with a heavy tax burden on the one hand and having to look after several children on the other. In an extended flash back in the novel, the divorced protagonist is shown as ending up with being a married woman, longing for mutual understanding and communication with her husband.

In sharp contrast, Akilon's autobiographical novels *Koḷḷaikkāran and Pāvai Viḷakku* present the full personality of the novelist as a boy, a student, a son, a lover, a husband, a father, a middle-aged middle-class government employee and a creative writer. Through the lives of Akilon's protagonists the readers manage to get glimpses of several experiences of his childhood, the middle years and the ripe years of maturity.

In the case of Sahgal's *The Day in Shadow* only the "motif" may be defined as autobiographical and not the character of the protagonist Simrit. Sahgal herself acknowledges this fact in her interview to Jasbir Jain in a highly self-conscious observation:

> *The Day in Shadow*...was based on a very definite experience of divorce and settlement with which I was landed and on that I based the novel but otherwise the woman I felt was not like me in the sense that at heart I have always been rebellious...whereas Simrit, I think was a supine kind of character...a sort of a docile woman.... I have never seen her as being as autobiographical character (177).

As against this, in most of Akilon's autobiographical novels not only the "motifs" but characters too are recreated from the episodes and personalities from real life. His protagonists in such novels are idealistic, adventurous, industrious, passionate, individualistic and optimistic like their creator. In these by and large romantic works, Akilon himself is at the centre, deliberately assuming different garbs and roles from one work to another.

The primary "motif" of Sahgal's *The Day in Shadow* constitutes the "stuff" of most of her novels. Not only Simrit but many other of Sahgal's characters like Maya in *A Time to Be Happy*, Rashmi in *This Time of Morning*, Saroj in *Storm in Chandigarh*, Nadira in *A Situation in New Delhi*, Rose and Mona in *Rich Like Us*, Lulu Croft in *Plans for Departure* and Bhushan's mother in her latest novel *Mistaken Identity* long for reciprocal relationship with their husbands on a mature assumption of mutual respect and equal dignity. It is, by and large, the recurrence of the "stuff" that eventually proves to be Sahgal's own undoing as a creative writer, for after the initial introduction to the theme of her novels, most readers grow sufficiently aware of what they are to expect from the rest of her works. But in Akilon's novels there is no tiresome repetition of any of his remarkable experiences from life. Each of his works has its own measure of raw material taken from Akilon's life and so there is a great deal of variety in respect of his "motif." Besides, Akilon had a much vaster repertoire of observations and experiences at his command, and it is this variety of raw material or "stuff" renders his autobiographical novels more rewarding.

From the above study, it is also evident that the two writers have their own way of reworking the events and personages from their personal lives into art. It is also true that Sahgal and Akilon as creative artists experience "life" differently in terms of their art as René Wellek rightly points out:

> A work of art may rather embody the dream of an author than his actual life, or it may be the 'mask,' the 'anti-self' behind which his real person is hiding or it may be a picture of the life from which the author wants to escape…the artist may experience 'life' differently in terms of his art (178).

NOTES

(i) With regard to transliteration of the titles of Akilon's works and other works in Tamil the notation set forth in the following text *The Journal of The Institute of Asian Studies*. 7.2, March 1990, has been followed in this paper. The system of transliteration adopted here is given below:

A System of Transliteration of Tamil

VOWELS

Short				Long	
அ	a			ஆ	ā
இ	i			ஈ	ī
உ	u			ஊ	ū
எ	e	ஐ	ai	ஏ	ē
ஒ	o	ஔ	au	ஓ	ō

CONSONANTS

Hard		Soft		Medial	
க்	k	ங்	ṅ	ய்	y
ச்	c	ஞ்	n̄	ர்	r
ட்	ä	ண்	ṇ	ல்	l
த்	t	ந்	n	வ்	v
ப்	p	ம்	m	ழ்	l
ற்	r	ன்	n	ள்	ḷ
ஸ்	s	ஷ்	s	ஹ்	ḥ
		ஜ்	j		

(ii) Translation of all passages quoted from Akilon's novel and other critical texts in Tamil have been mine.

WORKS CITED

Akilon. *Kataik Kalai* (Madras: Paari Puthakap Pannai, 1972).

——. *Koḷḷaikkāran.* 2nd ed. (Madras: Porkodi Veliydu, 1973).

——. *Eluttum Vālkkaiyum* 2nd ed. (Madras: Paari Puthakap Pannai, 1984).

Jain, Jasbir. "Establishing Connections: An Interview." *Nayantara Sahgal* (Jaipur: Printwell, 1994).

John, Usha. "Nayantara Sahgal," *Femina.* 4 Feb. 1972: 13.

Ramalingam, M. *Akilonin Kalaiyum Karuttum* (Madras: Tamil Puthaklayam, 1974).

Sahgal, Nayantara. *From Fear Set Free* (Delhi: Hind Pocket Books, 1970).

——. *The Day in Shadow* (New Delhi: Penguin Books India, 1971).

——. "Of Divorce and Hindu Woman," *The Hindustan Times*, 12 Dec. 1971.

—— and E.N. Mangat Rai (Ju.au). *Relationship: Extracts from a Correspondence* (New Delhi: Kali for Women, 1994).

Weisstein, Ulrich. *Comparative Literature and Literary Theory: Survey and Introduction* (London: Indiana UP, 1973).

Wellek, René and Austen Warren. *Theory of Literature* (Great Britain: Penguin Books, 1968).

9

Katherine Mansfield's *The Garden Party* and *At the Bay*—An Overview

SUMITA NASKER

KATHERINE MANSFIELD was an intensely involved person with a keen power of observation. She evolved a deeper and more inclusive view of life not through reading and discussing any great philosopher but by collating her own experiences and developing a coherent attitude of her own to live by. Mansfield's *The Garden Party* collection is an attempt to work out her understanding of the ambivalence of life and death. Elizabeth Bowen is correct in pointing out that, "we are to marvel at the persistent strength with which Katherine Mansfield, the artist, threw off the sick-room. She was conscious only of her vocation."[1] In fact, Bowen's opinion may be considered together with Katherine Mansfield's pronouncement, in her Journal of November, 1921: "It is only by acknowledging that I, being what I am, had to suffer this in order to do the work I am here to perform...by being thankful that work was not taken away from me..." (272). Mansfield's work is a part, a very vital part of her psychic evolution. Her stories, especially those included in her last book, illustrate her feeling of joy and tenderness towards external nature; as is her love of life itself. As she says:

> I am always wanting to lift the handkerchief off lizards' faces and pansies' faces and the house by moonlight. I am always wanting to put a blessing on what I see...[2] (Letter of October 7, 1920).

This urge to bless is the result of Katherine's acknowledgment of the valid and valued existence of all that is ugly (the lizard) and the beautiful (the pansy). This affirmation of the multifarious nature of life, Katherine had already spoken about in another letter, this time to Sylvia Lynd, written on January 31, 1920. Here she writes:

> All this self-examination, this hovering on the brink—it's all wrong: I don't believe a writer can ever do anything worth doing until he has—in the profoundest sense of the word—accepted life....[3]

Mansfield's final collection, *The Garden Party and Other Stories* is ample proof of her acceptance of life. The book shows that the author had, indeed, come to terms with life. Considering this it is hardly surprising that death and loneliness brood over the stories in this last book. Laura, in *The Garden Party,* is bewildered to discover that in the midst of a blissful, sheltered life delighted with its parties, death intrudes in the shape of the accidental demise of a poor carter. In *At the Bay,* the grandmother ponders over the untimely death of her son. Whilst, little Kezia thinks, "She didn't want to die" (39), for it meant leaving, "everywhere" and also her beloved grandma. In another story, "The Stranger," the husband realises that his wife has achieved an emotional attachment with the stranger who had died in his wife's arms. In "The Voyage" no one dies, but little Fenella Crane's journey to her grandfather's house is the result of her mother's death. In Mansfield's favourite story, "The Daughters of the Late Colonel," the entire narrative revolves around the two lonely, middle-aged sisters and their pathetic condition after the death of their domineering father. "Mr. and Mrs. Dove" is not about death. Nevertheless, Mansfield refers to the death of the central character's uncle Alick (123), who had left the fruit farm to his nephew. In "Marriage à La Mode," too, there is no demise but the focus is on the death of feelings, of love and tenderness—a wife, who has changed for the worse and fails to respond to the loving husband. Three other stories,—"An Ideal Family," "The Young Girl," and "Her First Ball"—deal with the theme of youth and old age. Whereas, "Miss Brill" paints a picture of solitude; the elderly spinster in this story can only look forward to a bleak existence. As the monologist in "The Lady's Maid" speaks, we are allowed glimpses of a lonely and exploited life in the clutches of her family and selfish employer. "The Singing Lesson" begins with the strains of loneliness and throughout "Bank Holiday" we perceive the happiness of a crowd captured on a beautiful day. The charwoman in the story, "Life of Ma Parker," is unable to fathom why her little grandson has to die after acute suffering. Her questions, "why must it all have happened to me?" and "what have I done?" (151) are rather suggestive. The second question is posed in Mansfield's letter to Middleton Murry, dated November 30, 1919,—"what have I done that I should have all the handicaps—plus a disease...." But in this letter, Katherine does add, "...really, I'd better get used to it."[4]

An examination of at least two of these stories included in *The Garden Party* collection will reveal they are products of Katherine Mansfield's integrated outlook. This final volume communicates, through the events delineated in the stories and the characters reactions, the diversity of existence. The events in themselves are not earth-shaking but significant in the lives of the fictional personages. After all, life consists of both important and unimportant happenings valuable to ordinary mortals. Katherine Mansfield's world is not peopled by kings and paupers. She is more concerned, more involved with the ordinary events in the lives of average human beings, who are so very close to us that their view of themselves and this globe, achieved during and after the events narrated, is enlightening for us. Mansfield does not preach any moral lesson but teaches us to see a little more deeply and more compassionately.

In the short story, "The Garden Party," Katherine Mansfield is not specifically drawing the picture of her own family but illustrating what she once suggested in a letter to Anne Estelle Rice, written in January 1921, "I try to make family life so gorgeous—not hatred and cold linoleum—but warmth and hydrangeas...."[5] Mr. Antony Alpers, in particular, suggested that the original garden party, on which the story is based, "could have been given at No. 75, Tinakori Road, with the weather safe and the girls in such hats..." in the early part of 1907, "for the Beauchamps left that house in April."[6] But this information does not enrich our understanding of the story. One must allow for the fact that the creative mind of the artist both consciously and unconsciously selects and heightens detail. The process is not one of falsification but of particular stress and here, this stress is primarily on family life, the inter-relationships of the members.

The story rather deceptively, seems to be simple and unsophisticated. In "The Garden Party," Mansfield's "selective camera"[7] focuses upon Laura, a young, vivacious and well-meaning girl trying her best to establish her own values in a world carefully arranged for her by her mother, Mrs. Sheridan, and her two elder sisters. The camera follows Laura as she adopts the ways of her mother in talking to the workmen, who have come with the marquee for the garden party; as Laura helps with the sandwiches, and as she confronts the insensitivity of her elders about the death of a poor neighbour. We observe her wavering loyalty to the attitude of her family and, on the other hand, to her instinctive youthful sense of humanity that makes Laura feel that the party ought to be cancelled as a mark of respect to the feelings of the afflicted family next-door. Mrs. Sheridan's employment of various devices to divert her daughter's independent point of view and to set her firmly once again in the Sheridan circle—are described. After the party, it is Mrs. Sheridan who suggests the idea of packing the party left-overs and sending Laura to the house of mourning, bearing the basket. One need not emphasise that this condescending gesture, so typical of Mrs. Sheridan, is objectionable since this is no ordinary visit to the house of poor folks, it is a bereaved family that Laura is asked to visit. But Laura's visit to Scott's house with the basket and her viewing of the dead body ultimately enables her to come to grips with reality.

The story, thus, centres around Laura and the afternoon affair is the first social occasion on which she is to play an adult role. It is, as critics have pointed out, her initiation into the mature world. Her family had considered her to be, "the artistic one" (66) and Laura, herself had, "...always felt she could do things,...much better than anybody else" (66). But the important question is, will Laura follow the foot-steps of her mother and become insensitive and artificial, or will she develop into a sensitive and compassionate person? The restricted view that Laura along with her sisters have been permitted by their mother has influenced her, as her conversation as well as her behaviour with the workers prove, "Laura's upbringing made her wonder for a moment whether it was quite respectful of a workman to talk to her of bangs slap in the eye" (67).

It is death that makes the difference—it forces this young girl to see in the older members of the Sheridan family the hardened views, which in Laura are still vague and indefinite imitations of adult models. Laura's knowledge of death means an end to innocence but it also heralds the possibility of the emergence of a new mind and selfhood. The demise of Scott, the carter, blocks the way for death of feelings in Laura—a death already suffered by all the other members of her family. Laura's initial reaction to the news of bereavement is one of shock, and this is accompanied by a strong demand for honesty and humane attitudes. To her sisters, "you won't bring a drunken workman back to life by being sentimental," she counters, "Drunk! who said he was drunk?" (78). Laura is similarly outraged when Mrs. Sheridan speaks nebulously of not understanding how the poor workers, "keep alive in those poky little holes" (79).

Although, the dead man is hardly a character in the story yet we are furnished with all the details about him—name, profession, address, the nature of his accident, the location of his wound, his marital status and the number of his children. This detailed information is essential to the breaking down in Laura of the vague barriers between classes. Laura's post-party trip to the dead man's house is then, a visit to a different world—a world of grief and misery which has a terrible face, "Her [Mrs. Scott's] face, puffed up, red, with swollen eyes and swollen lips, looked terrible. She seemed as though she couldn't understand why Laura was there..." (86). The young girl's discovery of new knowledge and new experiences proceeds further after the viewing of the corpse. Looking at the motionless body stretched out in front of her, Laura realises that this man is an inhabitant of another realm, which removed him, in a sense, from his slum world and also from her upper-class universe. The dead body is an occupant of another world away from the Sheridan's and the Scott's, and even Laura, herself.

It is hardly surprising that Laura's response to this new "marvel" should be a tearful, "Forgive my hat" (87). The awakened Laura's confrontation with death is frightening as well as an ecstatic experience. The author describes the young girl's perception of the grandeur of death; on the dead Scott's face there is an expression of bliss, of contentment.

It is a striking feature of Katherine Mansfield's art to conclude the story with an unfinished sentence, "Isn't life?" But what life was she couldn't explain" (87). Laura's sense of life is eventually beyond the reach of words. Nonetheless, a sympathetic brother, Laurie, with his warm, loving nature understands his sister and agrees with her, "'Isn't it, darling,' said Laurie" (87).

The story seems to suggest that life may not be as wonderful as death, and that death may be a way to peace and beauty. Death is at once terrible and beautiful. In life, the garden party and the death of a worker happen on the same day, at the same time of the day. Laura feels that such momentous happenings ought not to take place simultaneously. But they happen and it is inevitable, yet there is beauty in the inevitability.

Mansfield in a letter to William Garhardi written on March 13, 1922 (after the publication of the story) stated what her intention was in *The Garden Party.* She declared that the narrative exhibits:

> the diversity of life and how we try to fit into everything. Death included. That is bewildering for a person of Laura's age. She feels things ought to happen differently.... But life isn't like that....[8]

Indeed, life defies all attempts to put it in some order by any mortal.

In the story, *At the Bay*, the author concentrates on certain events taking place in the lives of the Burnell family. An incident in the life of Alice, the Burnell maid, is also included in the narrative. A noticeable feature of *At the Bay* is that, these events occur in twelve scenes or "Cells,"[9] as Ian Gordon calls them, and they all happen on a single day. Each scene revolves around the characters. They unearth a significant fact about themselves or about the world at large. The initial Scene (I) provides the setting for the central drama to unfold. The story begins with a picturesque description of an early morning: "when the sun was not yet risen, and the whole of Cresent Bay was hidden under white sea-mist" (9). Together with this, the description of the flowers, "the flufffy toi-toi," the "cold fuchsias," the marigolds, the gurgling "ferny basins," the shepherd with his flock, "myriads of birds" singing, not to forget the dog and Florrie, the cat (10)—contribute to the pictorial effect, which is another noticeable feature of Mansfield's stories. This description of nature places the characters in the context of time.

Then, from the next Scene (II) onwards, we encounter a series of revelations, both small and great, but important for the understanding of the diverse nature of existence. In this scene we come across a very trivial occurrence,—Stanley Burnell's annoyance at discovering that he was not the first person to bathe in the sea that morning, for his neighbour, Trout, was already in the water.

Mansfield, in a very subtle manner implies a contrast of these two men. This is clear from their behaviour. Trout's carefree nature is vividly conveyed by introducing him as gently floating in the water. Jonathan is a "trout" in water, taking life rather casually. Unlike the self-important Stanley, Trout preferred to, "take things easy...to live...basking in the light" (15), as the narrator explains to us. As the story proceeds we learn that Stanley is pompous because he is a successful man. Whilst, Trout is a mere office-clerk.

Scene III by taking us to the Burnell living-room shows Stanley unearthing a rather suggestive fact about his family. He feels that no one at home seems to really grasp the idea that he, Stanley Burnell, is the provider, the breadearner and he happens to be in dire straits because no one attached sufficient importance to the fact that he had to hurry to office. Mr. Stanley Burnell thinks that his own family did not rightly appreciate his importance and did not give him due regard. The instance in point is his realisation, "The way they took it for granted it was your job to slave away for them while they didn't even take the trouble to see that your walking-stick wasn't lost" (19).

The subsequent Scene (IV) focuses on the excitement of the Burnell girls and the Trout boys, on discovering what they consider to be "a nemeral" (25), (an emerald), on the sea-beach. Mansfield's ability to enter into the spirit of this discovery of the children is noticed in the way she makes Pip force the others to promise not to publicise his discovery and to, "say, cross my heart straight dinkum" (25), which all the girls repeat after him. This gives the impression that the author certainly knew exactly how children and adults behave in a family. Even if we notice children behaving in such a manner, most of us take these things for granted and do not even think about them. In this scene as well as in Scene IX we find Mansfield penetrating further into the recesses of childhood. In Scene IV Isabel's point of view indicates that, "aunt Beryl had a nemeral ring, but it was a very small one" (25). This again throws light on Isabel's power of observation and we feel that she, with her superior ideas, would be the only child to note the difference in the size of the stone. Isabel's sister Lottie, who fails to get over the stile and Kezia who shows her how to climb over and also takes up the cudgels on Lottie's behalf, are not concerned with the size of the precious stone. It is hardly surprising that their aunt Beryl is associated with this jewel, since her name, "Beryl," means a precious stone of which aquamarine and emerald are varieties. Marvin Magalaner in his book, *The Fiction of Katherine Mansfield,* informs us that, "the unusual name of Kezia is from the English 'Cassia' identifying a genus of shrubs and trees" and Kezia's mother, "has a name that recalls the Linden tree" ('Linda' in Old High German).[10]

In the following Scene (V) we are taken away from this innocent and credulous world of the children and transported to an adult world of corruption, suspicion and envy in and around Mrs. Harry Kember. This scene introduces us to the local gossip about the Bohemian Kembers, "he [Mr. Kember] ignored his wife just as she ignored him.... Of course there were stories... some of the women at the Bay privately thought he'd [Kember would] commit a murder one day..." (28). Mrs. Kember, is the strange looking woman, who incessantly smoked with a cigarette perpetually between her lips, while she conversed. Her allegedly nefarious activities are at first presented through the gossip about them. The narrator does not say anything specific about the Kembers. We view the mysterious, fascinating and seductive, Mrs. Kember, through Beryl's point of view. As Beryl overcomes her shyness and changes into her swimming costume she feels that she was being tempted, "she was being poisoned by this cold woman, but she [Beryl] longed to hear" (30-31). Beryl's opinion that Mrs. Kember was corrupting her may not be very reliable because her thoughts invariably border on things sensual. For instance, she thinks Alice was going into the bush with a "horrible larrikin" when Alice was only leaving for tea with Mrs. Stubbs (41). Even in *Prelude* we notice the presence of a hidden self within the carefree, external social self of Beryl, "It was her other self who had written that letter [to Nan Fry]. It was not only bored, it rather disgusted her real self" (58). In *At the Bay* (Scene V) Mrs. Kember openly admires Beryl's body and suggests, "Really, it is a sin for you to wear clothes, my dear" (30). But then, it is not quite palpable whether Mrs. Kember has plans to seduce or is seducing Beryl. In all probability the whole idea of corruption and seduction is a figment of Beryl's imagination. After all, she might have been influenced by the gossip of other women. Another reason could be Beryl's hidden self, which was easily tantalised. The emergence of this other self is noticeable in the final scene of *At the Bay.* Indeed, this young woman's discovery of Mrs. Kember's malevolent intentions and her own susceptibility is a prologue to the major insight that Beryl gains during her late night encounter with Mr. Harry Kember.

Scene VI belongs to introspective Linda Burnell immersed in her reverie under the manuka tree in the garden. Her daydream affords us with a view of those by-gone days when she dreamt of escaping, significantly, all the way to China in a boat (32), and the days when Stanley courted her. As Linda dreamt the morning away she found her, "real grudge against life" (33). This was her, "dread of having children" (33). Linda experienced a sense of relief because her infant son was looked after by her mother, "thank Heaven" (34). But, this indifferent mother soon realised, "There was something so quaint, so unexpected about that smile..." (34), of her son lying next to her, that she could not but respond to his antics, "...it was something so new, so...the tears danced in her eyes" (35). The moment Linda leaned over her baby she was, astonished at the confidence of this little creature..." (35), who seemed to mockingly say to its mother, "'don't like babies?' The boy couldn't believe her" (35). Linda thinks that her baby gave the impression that, "He didn't believe a word she said" (35). This establishes a rapport with the baby and the mother then lovingly addresses it as, "'Hallo, my funny'" (35). But, by now the baby's attention was focused on something else that waved in front of him. This scene highlights Linda's discovery that her attitude may be "mocked" by a baby and a baby can be an amused companion at one moment and utterly indifferent at the next.

The next Scene (VII) draws our attention to little Kezia's discovery. Kezia fathoms the central fact of life that some day we all have to die and our permission will not be sought. It is grandmother, Fairfield's walk down memory lane and her meditation on the death of her son, which helps Kezia to learn about this mystery of existence. In this scene Mansfield introduces us to Kezia's point of view, "...over there on the weed-hung rocks that looked like shaggy beasts...the sunlight...danced, they quivered...the vast mountainous country behind those houses—the raviness,...fearful tracks that led to the water's edge..." (36). In this passage the viewpoint of a small child seeing objects larger than herself, rendered even larger and fearful by her imagination is recorded. We read another full page before Kezia appears in person. But she is already present for we have approached the beach throught her eyes.

Along with Kezia's viewpoint we are furnished with the grandmother's point of view, "It was the old woman's turn to consider. Did it [her son's death] make her sad? To look back, back" (38). Mansfield, by using shifting points of view in this scene is able to show us the emotional dependence of the grandchild on her own grandmother. The author has also given as the point of view of the narrator as in, "Kezia and her grandmother was taking their siesta together..." (37).

An invitation to tea, a minor happening in the life of Alice, in Scene VIII, makes her feel, that even the choicest delicacies on the table, "ham, sardines, a whole pound of butter and such a large johnney cake..." (43), together with her hostess's entertaining ability, cannot prevent her (Alice) from wishing to go back to her, "own kitching" (45).

In this scene, the late Mr. Stubbs is described as having been carried off by dropsy. Rather than mourning his passing, Mrs. Stubbs shocks Alice by insisting that, "freedom's best" (45). This is a wife's reaction to the death of her husband and this is implicitly contrasted with a mother's (Mrs. Fairfield's) response to her son's death and also with Kezia's idea of the cessation of life, "you're not to die" declares a very "decided" Kezia to her grandma (39). The very idea of departure is heart-wrenching to this little girl. Thus, the author's use of juxtaposition is noted.

Again, in Scene VIII, it is the narrator who points out that aunt Beryl was erroneous ("un-fair") in assuming that the dressed up Alice was going off into the bush with, "some horrible larrikin" (41). But in two other stories, "The Garden Party" and "The Doll's House," consideration of the feelings of the unfortunate ones is expressed through the central characters, Laura and Kezia, compared to them, Beryl's mind is obsessed with thoughts of corrupt sensuality around herself. She flirts with her own brother-in-law, Stanley, in "Prelude" and in *At the Bay*, she decides to take a night walk with a married man.

Besides, in *At the Bay* we perceive the narrator laughing at Mrs. Stubbs. This is evident when the hostess, Mrs. Stubbs, tried to entertain her guest, Alice, with the roar of her primus-stove drowning their conversation. Even in Mrs. Stubbs' description of the disease (dropsy) we find the narrator making fun of her, "...here Mrs. Stubbs creaked and seemed to expand herself at the memory..." (44).

The reference to the fading of the gorgeous daylight in the west, in Scene IX, brings to mind the passage of time. This is the time of the day which heralds the mysterious in the presence of the children engaged in playing cards and pretending to be different kinds of animals in the washhouse, "...the perfect place for them, because they could make as much noise as they liked..." (45-46). But darkness descended and no one came to take them home. The very idea of this alleged abandonment culminates in a piercing scream; for it is unthinkable to the young minds that grown-ups can forget about them.

We remember Katherine Mansfield's children—Kezia, Rags, Lottie, "Our Else" and the Samuel Josephs because, she had that purity of vision which enabled her to enter into their lives without sentimentality, without condescending or patronising them. Charles Dickens, too, possessed this ability to become a child for the moment and to view the world with the eyes of the child (as in the first thirteen chapters of *David Copperfield*). Arthur Sewell in his essay on Mansfield is correct in suggesting that, "...the best comment ever made on Katherine Mansfield's stories was, 'Gosh! Those kids are real.'"[11] One is also reminded of George Shelton Hubbell's striking observation, "Katherine Mansfield is a prophet, a prophet of children.... Katherine Mansfield respects children...it is exceedingly rare...."[12] Many of Mansfield's critics have also commented on Kezia's affinity with the author. Both Mr. Alpers[13] and Jeffrey Meyers[14] have noted this affinity in their works, for example, Meyers refers to Kezia as, "the autobiographical child."

The tenth (X) episode of *At the Bay* gives prominence to Linda's understanding of Jonathan Trout. Along with her, we too, perceive that Trout had intentionally chosen the, "nine to five" life of an office-goer (when his talents lay elsewhere). Trout was of a lethargic disposition, his rudderless mode of living is of his own making, as he divulges, "I put myself in jail [office] and nobody's ever going to let me out..." (53). We learn about the hidden potential in Jonathan Trout's nature through Linda's grasp of the "intolerable situation" (53) in which the musically inclined Trout had placed himself.

In some of Mansfield's short stories, we detect that the true self of an individual is often deliberately distorted, even life or environment or circumstances frequently hamper the blossoming of this true self. Here, Trout seems to be full of self-pity. He is able to sum up his character in very precise terms. In fact, Trout clearly sees his own situation, "scratching in somebody's ledger. It's a queer use to make of one's abilities" (55). Nonetheless, he is weak, lacking any stamina to change the course of his life. He admits that he is too "old" (56) to change anything. The restrictions that old age places on man is appropriately underlined when Linda sees that, Trout is, "...not resolute...but touched already with age" (56). In Linda's judgment of Trout lies the author's superb use of irony. Linda, who is always miles away from this world and spends her time dreaming, she, is the only person to discover that Trout is not determined but already, touched with age. She discerns the onslaught of time on man.

In Scene XI, the long day's end and the rumble of the coach bringing Mr. Stanley Burnell home from his office, prepares us for the events of the night. On returning home, Stanley confesses to the surprised Linda, that he, "had a hell of a day...I've been in tortures..." (57) simply because he hurriedly went away without kissing his wife goodbye. Stanley is shocked to learn that his wife has quite forgotten about this.

But the languid Linda is oblivious of Stanley's feelings and is interested in the new gloves that he is holding in his hands, "what's that you've got in your hand?" (58). Instead of answering Stanley's question, Linda asks one question in return. Thereby, changing the topic of the conversation.

We fathom that even in Stanley's gesture of affection there is a tinge of pomposity. He is making a scene about his wife's forgetfulness. Even when he announces that he had been suffering the entire day for not kissing Linda, he had been, "sensible" enough to purchase gloves for himself. This is another instance of Mansfield's use of irony. The concluding sentences of this scene, "Stanley wanted to say, 'I was thinking of you the whole time I bought them'...but for some reason he couldn't say it..." (58), denote Stanley's awareness of the falsity of uttering such a preposterous thing. The fact that he bought the gloves for himself, shows that he is concerned with his own thoughts and feelings. He is wrapped up in his world as Linda is submerged in her dreamland.

In spite of the author's use of irony in this scene, we recognise that only in the New Zealand stories (like "Prelude" and *At the Bay*) Mansfield deals with a happy marriage (of the Burnells), elsewhere (in "The Escape" or in "Bliss") the husband-wife relationship stresses the idea of incompatibility.

The final event of the day described by Mansfield in the last Scene (XII) is the most disturbing manifestation in the story, *At the Bay.* Beryl steps into the garden to have an adventure with a married man. Beryl, whose main complaint in "Prelude" is that she is isolated from life, imprisoned in the new house in the suburbs, exposes herself to the dangers of life. Harry Kember suggests the idea of the walk when, "...There's not a soul about" (60). Though Beryl hesitated initially yet there is no indication of her firmly putting her foot down. Mansfield uses the image of the snake to emphasise the emergence of the hidden self of Beryl, "who shook her head. But already something stirred in her, something reared its head. The voice said, 'Frightened.' It mocked, 'Poor little girl'" (62). As Beryl spoke out aloud that she was not frightened at the prospect, the narrator suggests, "As she spoke that weak thing within her seemed to uncoil, to grow suddenly tremendously strong; she longed to go" (62). Beryl's longing indicates that she permitted herself to be driven by suppressed desires. But suddenly, she withdrew, "No, I'm not coming any farther" (63). Herein, lies the clash of the real self with the external self of Beryl. The concealed self of Beryl desired much but these urges were consciously kept in check by the social exterior. The moment she extricated herself from the embrace of Harry Kember, she shouted, "you are vile, vile" (64). But in one sense Beryl is "vile." She lacks the courage to go the whole way; she had agreed to go for a walk and she did step into the garden. "...now she was here she was terrified..." (63). Beryl is scared owing to the longings stirring within her; along with this is the feeling of guilt. The intrusion of her social, "respectable" self results in Beryl running away to the house leaving Harry Kember stammering, "Then, why in God's name did you come?" We feel that this man was only doing what was expected from him in the given situation.

The concept of the two selves, the concealed and the unconcealed, is referred to in several letters of Mansfield. In a letter to Middleton Murry, Mansfield informs him:

> There are still traces of what I call your sham personality in this book...the personality that expressed itself in the opening paragraphs of your Santayana review in *The Nation.*[15]

To her friend, Ida Baker, she frankly admits:

> I take advantage of you—demand perfection of you.... A deeper self looks at you and a deeper self in you looks back and we laugh and say, 'what nonsense.'[16]

Mansfield's belief in the presence of different selves within an individual is also confirmed from certain statements made in her Journal. In her Journal of April 1920 she affirms:

> Our persistent yet mysterious belief in a self which is continuous and permanent; which untouched by all we acquire and all we shed...the light discovers it.... When we are most ourselves and least personal.[17]

Indeed, it is interesting to note that Mansfield recognised the presence of more than one self within her. This is evident from an entry in her *Scrapbook.* Under the caption "The Flowering of the Self" (136), we come across the following confession of the author, "...True to oneself: which self? Which of my many—well, really, that's what it looks like coming to—hundreds of selves?" (*Scrapbook* 136).

Furthermore, in *At the Bay,* Mansfield is mainly occupied with the happenings on one day in the life of the Burnell family, just as Virginia Woolf draws our attention to a single day in the life of Mrs. Dalloway (in the novel, *Mrs. Dalloway*). In both cases the time present is just as important as the time passed. Walter Allen suggests that Mrs. Woolf's novel shows, "...life is in a state of constant creation, changing endlessly from moment to moment, like a fountain...."[18] In Mansfield's story, the time passed, Linda's childhood, Stanley's courtship (32-33), and grandmother Fairfield looking back, thinking about her son, Walter (38), are brought in. Here too, life is continuous, and the past goes on living in the present. But Mansfield's short story was composed in 1921 when *Mrs. Dalloway* was not even written.

REFERENCES

1. *Stories,* selected and with an Introduction by Elizabeth Bowen (1956; rpt. New York: Vintage-Knopf, 1987), xx.
2. See *The Letters of Katherine Mansfield,* Vol. II, 51.
3. *Ibid.,* 9.
4. See *The Letters of Katherine Mansfield,* Vol. I, 307.
5. This letter of January, 1921, addressed to A.E. Rice was printed in *Adam International Review,* no. 300, London, 1965, 93.
6. Antony Alpers. *The Life of Katherine Mansfield* (OUP, 1980) 46.

7. A.R. Orage. *Selected Essays and Critical Writings,* (ed.) Herbert Read and Denis Saurat (London: Stanley Nott, 1935) 129. Orage reports Mansfield as having told him: "I've been a camera...a selective camera, and it has been my attitude that has determined the selection; with the result that my slices of life...have been partial, misleading, and a little malicious."
8. See *The Letters and Journals,* 259. In this letter Mansfield also states: "And it seems to me there is beauty in that inevitability."
9. See *Undiscovered Country: The New Zealand Stories of Katherine Mansfield,* (ed.) Ian Gordon (London: Longmans, 1974) xix, states: "The structure of Katherine's stories after 1915 abandons the somewhat mechanical progression of events of her earlier work. She herself called the new structure 'the *Prelude* method—it just unfolds and opens.' The stories are organic and not mechanical in structure, multi-cellular like living tissue. *Prelude* has twelve such 'cells,' as has *At the Bay. The Stranger* has two. Other stories have a single-cell structure.... There is little 'plot,' in the traditional sense, but as each cell 'unfolds and opens' the reader is brought in to share the life of the family."
10. Marvin Magalaner. *The Fiction of Katherine Mansfield* (U.S.A.: Southern Illinois UP, 1971) 32.
11. Arthur Sewell. *Katherine Mansfield: A Critical Essay* (Auckland, New Zealand: Folcroft Library Editions, 1972) 28-29.
12. G.S. Hubbell. "Katherine Mansfield and Kezia" in *The Sewanee Review,* (U.S.A., July — September 1927) 325-26, states: "Plato regarded children as future citizens, hence material to be worked on by the states. Dickens thought the little darlings should be wept and gushed about.... Wordsworth made them the text for a philosophy of life.... But Samuel Butler held that children are human beings, and Katherine Mansfield insists upon treating them as such...."
13. Alpers 190, states: "The child Kezia is central, as we'd expect. She is kass, of course...."
14. Jeffrey Meyers. *Katherine Mansfield: A Biography* (London: Hamish Hamilton, 1978) 128.
15. See *The Letters and Journals of Katherine Mansfield,* 206.
16. *Ibid.*, 259.
17. John Middleton Murry (ed.). *Journal of Katherine Mansfield* (London: Constable, 1954) 205.
18. Walter Allen. *The Modern Novel* (New York: E.P. Dutton, 1964) 17.

10

From Courtyards to Horizons: A Reading of Anjana Appachana's "Her Mother" and Shani Mootoo's "A Garden of Her Own"

AMEENA K. ANSARI

ANJANA APPACHANA'S "Her Mother" and Shani Mootoo's "A Garden of Her Own" are stories that delve into the matrix of identity politics foregrounded through the creative medium of the word. As the creative expressions of diasporic writers, they revolve round that particular brand of immigrant experience which focuses on the interiorisation of memory "by exploring new areas of meaning and new possibilities of consciousness" (Devy 8). The protagonists go down memory lane and their consciousness is shown to crystallize meaning from these memories. In "Her Mother," the mother is able to finally grasp the compulsions that drove her beloved younger daughter, Rani beti, to study in the United States; in "A Garden of Her Own," Vijai, the young bride has to seek her own identity as an immigrant trapped in a stifling marriage. Both stories emanate from the immigrant experience of transition from the warm, tropical climes of Asia to the cold, temperate world of North America. In this topographical shift are implicated the emotional odysseys of the protagonists. The knives of memory cut through their passive existence and goad them into seeking and asserting their identities. Though these narratives are born out of life's ordinariness, they reflect what Meenakshi Mukherjee, in *Realism and Reality*, calls the "willed tendency of art to approximate reality" (16) that is gender specific. This is double dependence or the dual roles that they have to play as woman on one side and daughter/wife on the other. They begin as narratives that portray the emergence of culturally trapped women's voices which are marked by the sense of loneliness and alienation. These embody the stark realities of the expatriate female experience, which both stories reiterate, thereby foregrounding the sense of being hemmed within a metaphorical, mental courtyard beyond which the horizon of freedom and self-realisation constantly beckons.

The courtyard/horizon tussle is rooted in two basic dilemmas that assail the migrant's consciousness, whether it be a man or a woman. One has to do with the choice or conflict between the traditional concept of duty, which is ingrained in minds of Asians, especially those from our subcontinent, as part and parcel of the cultural milieu which they can choose to leave behind, and the Western one of the pursuit of happiness in the milieu that they have chosen to go to. The second choice or conflict concerns the passionate desire of making it financially or professionally in an environment that is dominated by consumerism. In both these spheres of choice, the female migrant treads warily, having to negotiate between the ideal (which is linked to cultural roots of her past) and the actual (which should translate as a success story in a new land). In "Her Mother," the unmarried daughter chooses to reject familiar obligations (after her brief incestuous liaison with her brother-in-law) and flees to America in the pursuit of happiness which selfishly precludes anyone other than herself. In adopting this course of action, she stresses her passionate yearning for making it academically by pushing emotional trauma into cobwebby attics of memory. In "A Garden of Her Own," Vijai's marital isolation and crisis is exacerbated by frequent bouts of memory and guilt that stress her inability to conform to the standards of marital duty ingrained in her by her mother. Ultimately, she seeks her own equilibrium of happiness by indulging in her hobby of gardening and watching francophone Canada's television programmes which symbolise companionship in a place where she feels like a foreigner.

In both the stories, the initial phase of self-pity is replaced by a spurt of individualism which is instrumental in propelling the protagonists towards self-realisation and/or self-reliance. It is the evolution of this spirit which transmutes both the stories into narratives of resistance and empowerment born of a fictional analysis of isolation and alienation. The brooding tone of isolation and alienation pervades the two narratives in which the figure of the mother predominates the cycle of events and memory. She is the stereotypical creation which needs no first or family name—she is seen flitting through the narrative in her biological role as the one who nurtures offspring, simultaneously endeavouring to placate her spouse through a myriad servile ways that only stress her position as the second sex.

It is in the narrative technique that the points of divergence emerge. "Her Mother" is a synthesis of the epistolary and stream-of-consciousness narrative. The mother is shown to have flashes of revelation when memory, mind and imagination combine to derive meanings from situations which, till then, her eyes had only superficially scanned. The pieces of her memory's jigsaw puzzle fall into place when she remembers the midnight snacks prepared by her daughter, Rani Beti, and the brother-in-law, the former holding this man's soiled kerchief against her face, the girl's sudden cutting off of her thick tresses and subsequent withdrawal into an uncommunicative shell from which she never emerged. The climactic moment comes when all these memories merge and then re-emerge in the mother's mind as definitive pointers to the incestuous physical intimacy shared by unmarried daughter and brother-in-law. She knows with certainty then that Rani beti will never return from America where she has fled from a restricted, reductive and, thereby, traumatic existence as a woman whose body had been defiled and then cast away. As a mother in New Delhi, she now understands that while one kind of angst has compelled her daughter to flee, another confronts the girl who faces life as an alien in land that has no emotional or cultural support systems to offer.

Mootoo's "A Garden of Her Own" resorts to retrospective sweeps of memory juxtaposed with acutely painful perceptions of the present. Vijai is constantly driven to compare and contrast the asphyxiating quality of her marital life in the West with the protective warmth of her pre-marital status in her parental home. The mother figures predominantly in Vijai's memories of the past, especially during occasions when she is involved in domestic chores. Each time Vijai thinks of transgressing the hammered-in code of conduct that her mother had ingrained in her, she is overcome by guilt. After having had to eat many congealed meals that had hardened to a candle-wax finish because her spouse was too busy trying to make it in life as an immigrant, Vijai defiantly decides not to wait for him and instead eats first. This very thought conjures up the image of a disapproving maternal glance. Aghast at the temerity of a daughter daring to do such a thing, these incidents compel Vijai to think in terms of formulating her own code of marital ethics that would negate her training of subservience as a wife and would help her to evolve a self-identity better equipped to deal with an indifferent marriage.

Both Appachana and Mootoo consciously take recourse to shattering the mother-myths of our subcontinent by bestowing on their fictional daughters the hyperactive mechanisms of emotional resurgence after their particularly traumatic interactions with indifferent men. The glaring contrast between the attitudes of the mothers and the daughters serves to emphasise their predilections as women of the metaphorical courtyard or the horizon. The canon of the courtyard demands that women keep away from strange, friendly men, do not stray too far away from the protective custody of parents or husbands, perfect the art of domestic chores, revel in keeping long tresses that serve to highlight the presentability and beauty of the wearer, and keep dreaming of a prince charming guaranteed to bestow love, jewellery and silks if they meet the other perquisites.

The older generation typifies a courtyard mentality that is invariably introverted and inward-looking. Within the confinement of their marital homes, and despite their claims to a liberal formal education, these women prioritise the needs of their spouses and emerges as *sati-savitris* whose very *raison d'être* are their husbands. They revel in the knowledge that they are the household deities without whom their spouses would be disoriented and lost. The mother in "Her Mother" recalls how her husband "could never find his clothes, slept on the bedcover, constantly misplaced his spectacles, didn't know how to get himself a glass of water and kept waiting for the postman" (Appachana 186) each time she went to visit her parents. In "A Garden of Her Own," Vijai remembers her mother's obsessive supervision of meals that were rituals beginning with intricate flower arrangements, summoning her four children to the table to eat together and ending with her staying hungry for days when her spouse deigned not to make an appearance. The roles of these mothers are so stereotypical of enclosure that the writers have no hesitation in dispensing with the norm of giving them actual names. Their generic reference—"mother"—is succinct and pertinent to their roles as inmates of real, as well as, metaphorical courtyards in which they choose not to play out their lives but also endeavour to spatially, as well as emotionally, confine their daughters.

The younger generation of women, as portrayed by Appachana and Mootoo, also begin life within metaphorical courtyards constructed by their mothers. As their memories reach back into the past, both Rani beti of "Her Mother" and Vijai in "A Garden of Her Own" are acutely aware of their roles they are expected to play as women. Their early training is one befitting the daughter of the house but this undergoes a subtle deviation when they reach a marriageable age. At this phase in life, they are expected to be groomed in the art of docility. It is this juncture in the lives of the protagonists that both Appachana and Mootoo chose to focus upon. This relates to an ingrained norm of conduct that is characteristic of the subtle codes and conventions steeped in the age-old ideals of womanly compromise, adjustment and adaptability, and most importantly, silence even in the direst of straits. Both Rani beti and Vijai become victims of this mode of existence. The former bears the brunt of her mother's training which taught her deference to male relatives, and she gets caught up in an intimate physical relationship with her brother-in-law who subscribes to an Epicurean way of life. Vijai's training compels her to be silent victim of violation in a marriage where no emotional bonds exist. Both girls are driven to despair in these wretched relationships. After initial hesitation, both protagonists mentally map out possible routes of escape from the oppressive confinement of their interaction with men. They emphatically reject and overthrow the maternal idealism of the courtyard and look towards horizons of possibility that will rejuvenate them. Their actions underline, through protest, the gynocentric thrust of the two narratives. The stories can be read as discourses which revolve around the cultural, biological and psychological shades of gynocentricism. It is in these pivotal spheres of existence that the protagonists have had to endure the sense of enclosure in their past; it is from them that they decide to seek a clean break. Like the symbolic phoenix, they choose to rise from the ashes of a bitter past marked by the loss of self-esteem. They seek renewal as women ready to plunge again into the problematic of life. But before this they take recourse to a ritualistic renunciation and effacement of their former selves, Rani beti chooses to actually snip off her knee-length tresses which had been greatly admired by her brother-in-law; Vijai only contemplates similar action.

It is interesting to note this common mode of self-effacement chosen by Rani beti and Vijai. It reflects the "Rapunzel" syndrome (Atwood 209) which transcends all national boundaries. The cutting of Rapunzel's hair in the fairy tale marks the end of her stepmother's domination over her and terminates in her union with her rescuer, the Prince. The female protagonist is the fictional equivalent of Rapunzel imprisoned in a tower by her wicked stepmother. Considered from a contemporary perspective, it is the mother or husband who assumes the role of the jailer; repressive mores within society or culture symbolise the metaphorical tower of imprisonment from which the Rapunzel/protagonist figure yearns to escape; and this escape is usually facilitated by a rescuer who provides only temporary respite. Rani beti's brother-in-law and Vijai's husband play the role of the rescuers bestowing short-lived relief from the oppressive courtyard personified by the mother. Repressed sexuality and its release prefigures as an essential component of the Rapunzel/courtyard realities. It manifests itself in "Her Mother" through the commuting marriage of Rani beti's sister in Bombay and her brother-in-law in Delhi; it also has reverberations in her action of holding her brother-in-law's soiled kerchief tenderly against her face. In "A Garden of Her Own," Vijai unsuccessfully attempts to seduce her husband into gentle lovemaking but ends up either as a victim of unwarranted indifference or of violent physical brutalisation. As these rescuers ironically evolve into forces of repression, the Rapunzel/protagonist has to once again seek refuge. This time, however, the avenues of refuge emerge from within the protagonist. Backed by steely will-power, Rani beti and Vijai rest faith in themselves and resolve to seek their emotional equilibrium in alternative action rather than people. The former decides in favour of a life of academia that is far removed from the orbits of her mother or brother-in-law. The latter indulges in the hobby of gardening to avoid incessant brooding and to keep herself appropriately pre-occupied. Even these resources are temporary as the niggling realities of being aliens in foreign land overcome them. Once again they are overwhelmed by loneliness which leaves them comatose and indifferent to their environment. For Rani beti, "everything was fine, her plane journey, her professor, her university, her house, the teaching, and even herself" (Appachana 181). For a Ph.D. scholar in Comparative Literature, these perceptions were a remarkably pathetic summation of her existence as an immigrant. Vijai takes to watching "snowy black-and-white television...listening to a language (French) that she does not understand comforts her, gives her companionship in a place where she feels like a foreigner" (Mootoo 169). It is on this note that the "Her Mother" and "A Garden of Her Own" respectively end. These despondent comments of the two women embody their dual tragedy. Their voices are manifestations of the immigrant's interior exile marked by the absence of community living which, especially in the context of our subcontinent, is the cornerstone of life in society. Secondly, they reflect tragic undertones of a woman's life marked by the commodification of her body, the cultural enclosure of her sexual self, and the psychological assault on her mind.

Through the framework of a logocentric narrative, Appachana and Mootoo symbolically foreground contemporary currents in the debate on feminism and gender politics. The two stories subtly critique the concept of reflective gender solidarity that had found currency in 1970s and 1980s. They do not have anything to do with the theoretical conceptualisation of this position which foregrounds egalitarian talks of justice and power. Instead, both narratives seem to be exploring the notion of a kind of discursive universalism, or what Seyla Benhabib terms "solidaristic community which sustains one's identity through mutual recognition" (27). This outlook transcends all national/ cultural divides. It endeavours to redefine gender politics as identity politics. The subscribers to this outlook strive to find common ground or cross-cultural affinities that bind female experience across the globe. In seeking to independently construct their identities, Rani beti and Vijai transcend the limiting frontiers of memory, space and time. They become the symbolic fictional representatives of a trend that prioritises the issue of quest or odyssey as the mainspring that shapes and determines woman's identity. It is through the medium of experience, both enriching and traumatising, that the quest/ odyssey is undertaken. It finds its culmination in the achievement of selfhood for the undertaker. Though this implies that there are many quests/odysseys as there are women, or fictional characters seeking selfhood, it is amply clear that it is participation in such enterprise unites them. A writer's strength lies in persuading the reader to imagine what it is like to be somebody else. This holds true for Anjana Appachana's "Her Mother" and Shani Mootoo's "A Garden of Her Own" both of which emerge as narratives of discursive universalism that puts national/cultural divides on the back burner by focusing on the dreams of women who struggle to emerge from the courtyards of enclosure to nurture dreams and cope with the realities of the horizon.

WORKS CITED

Appachana, Anjana. "Her Mother" *The Inner Courtyard* (Calcutta: Rupa & Co., 1991).

Atwood, Margaret. *Survival* (Toronto: Anansi, 1972).

Benhabib, Seyla. *From Identity Politics to Social Feminism: A Plea for the Nineties.* Cornell UP, 1994.

Devy, G.N. "The Indian English Novel 1980-90: An Overview," *Indian English Fiction 1980-90* (Delhi: B.R. Publishing Corporation, 1994).

Mootoo, Shani. "A Garden of Her Own" *Out on Mainstreet and Other Stories* (Toronto: Press Gang, 1993).

Mukherjee, Meenakshi. *Realism and Reality: The Novel and Society in India.* (Delhi: OUP, 1985).

11

A Comparative Study of Santa Rama Rau's Play *A Passage to India* and E.M. Forster's Novel *A Passage to India*

VEENA NARE

IN THIS brief critical paper I would like to examine Santa Rama Rau's Play: *A Passage to India*, and compare it with its original novel by E.M. Forster: *A Passage to India*.

While doing this I would like to show how far it is a faithful rendering and dramatisation of the novel *A Passage to India*. In case there are some deviations from or distortions of the original novel, I would like to examine the scheme of Santa Rama Rau's play and E.M. Forster's novel fixing her responsibility for these shortcomings or distortions on the conscious level of writing the play.

A Student-Edition of the play by Santa Rama Rau (Oxford, 1976) with a critical commentary by Prof. V.A. Shahane will be examined in this paper. (This play was first published in 1960 and was staged first at Oxford Play House on 10th January 1960.)

On examining the play, I found that Santa Rama Rau has completely omitted the last and the most important movement of the original novel "Temple."

Her play begins in the living room of Principal Fielding's Bungalow, instead of in the Mosque, and ends immediately after the Court case is over, that is—when Dr. Aziz is declared "not guilty."

The concluding lines in her book are:

> The youngman working the punkha continues to twitch his foot, staring without expression over the empty court-room as the curtain falls.[1]

This clearly shows that the entire action in this play takes place in and around Chandrapore and its adjoining Marabar Caves.

Since Santa Rama Rau has dramatised only the first two movements: "Mosque" and "Caves" from the original novel on which the play is based, the readers or spectators of Rau's play would not know what happens to the characters in the last movement—"Temple."

So her scheme has disturbed the thematic and the aesthetic harmony of the original novel by E.M. Forster.

As, Santa Rama Rau's play is a partial rendering of its original, its borrowed title—"A Passage to India" is quite misleading. In fact, critics now, are busy examining the thematic range of E.M. Forster's novel, *A Passage to India.*

One critic Benita Parry in her essay, "Passage to More than India"[2] shows how the novel justifies its title in the light of Whitman's poem, "A Passage to India."

Let us examine now what a Forster critic Prof. V.A. Shahane has said about this play in his critical commentary in the Student-Edition of the play.

Prof. V.A. Shahane's commentary shows a patronising attitude to the writer Santa Rama Rau: "The limitations of dramatisation probably influenced Santa Rama Rau to omit altogether the third section 'Temple' (of Forster's novel) from the play."[3]

This was almost inevitable since the mystical perceptions of Godbole were too subtle and too abstract for a play of action and character. However, the omission goes counter to the modern interpretation of *A Passage to India* in which greater stress is being laid on the symbolic events in "Temple" than on the baffling episode of the Marabar Caves. Her choice is partly governed by the fact that the events in Caves are more manageable in a play than those in "Temple."[4]

I personally feel, Santa Rama Rau has failed to understand the relative significance of the last movement "Temple." She must have felt that the "Temple" is a kind of appendage to the novel and it could be easily dropped. This shows her poor dramatic insight. Her play has distorted the aesthetic and the thematic design of the original novel.

Santa Rama Rau could not communicate to the spectators/ readers the mystical and spiritual aspects of the two major characters Professor Godbole and Mrs. Moore.

Christopher Gillie in his book *A Preface to Forster* observes:

> Godbole and Mrs. Moore are the poles of the novel's axis: Godbole the learned Brahmin immersed so deeply in the mysteries of his religion that relationship with individuals seem meaningless to him, and Mrs. Moore the earnest Christian, for whom the centre of life's meaning is personal relations: Godbole who nevertheless ends with this mystical expression of inclusive love, and Mrs. Moore who ends up loving nobody, least of all herself. This seeming reversal of role is the deepest theme in the novel underlying, but not distinct from that of the relationship of other three characters....[5]

Mrs. Rau in her defence calls Drama "a coarser medium" and further says "Mrs. Moore is an unmanageable character."[6&7]

A test of a good rendering or translation lies in meeting the challenges in the text creatively and not in running away from those challenges.

Santa Rama Rau cleverly chose to escape meeting the great challenges in "Temple."

I fail to understand why Prof. V.A. Shahane ends his commentary with a quotation from a hastily written review in *The Times* (London) in that year:

> The appeal of Forster's novel is timeless because it encounters the baffling, human predicament. It is a classic because it opens the reader's passage to India and to more than India, that is the passage of man to God.

Santa Rama Rau's play projects this predicament dramatically and therefore it is indeed in the words of *The Times* (London), a "remarkable, sensitive and faithful rendering of the novel."[8]

This clearly shows how the critics in the early sixties were undecided about their stand on the Temple movement.

How can a play be "a faithful rendering of the novel" when it has completely omitted the most important movement Temple?

In 1962, E.M. Forster's famous interview changes the course of the criticism of *A Passage to India*:

> Interviewer: What was the exact function of the long description of the Hindu Festival in *A Passage to India*?
>
> Forster: It was architecturally necessary. I needed a lump, or a Hindu Temple if you like—a mountain standing up. It is well placed and it gathers up some strings. But there ought to be more after it. The lump, sticks out a little too much (Writers at work 27).

Then, critic after critic came forward to defend his stand on the significance of the last movement "Temple." Prof. V.A. Shahane very well knew the change in Forster criticism, for in his article "Search for a Synthesis" he has given us how Wilfred Stone, "has very ably demonstrated the architectural design of *A Passage to India*":

> The Temple is a symbol of a World-Mountain with a Cave at its heart. The cave is at the centre of this house of God just as it is at the centre of the novel....
>
> This view emphasises the prominent function of the third section of the novel, 'Temple.'[9]

In fact, in the same article he shows how he "had propounded a similar view of the dominant symbolism of 'Temple' in unfolding the meaning and significance of *A Passage to India* in an essay published in 1963."[10]

Then we have Phillippa Moody who also defends E.M. Forster's architectural necessity of Temple in her critical commentary on *A Passage to India*:

> "Altogether one must, I think, agree with Forster's own criticism of the last section of his novel, its architectural necessity is nevertheless apparent. The second chapter 'Caves' would not do as a conclusion; it is both too one-sided and too simplified. Fielding retreats to England, Aziz to a state under Hindu Rule; the Englishman and the Indian cannot after all, be friends. But the scope of the novel, as we have seen, has been much wider than the scope of that single problem. Forster must go somewhere after the Caves.[11]

Now I think I should conclude this article with the latest criticism on *A Passage to India* by Christopher Gillie, a former lecturer at Cambridge University:

> The last movement of the novel 'Temple' elucidates and allays personal antagonisms—Aziz's misunderstanding of Fielding and his hostility to Adela who is now in England. It also culminates the religious theme and the two themes are of course, closely related. The culmination as we might expect, comes chiefly through Professoer Godbole, and his performance in a religious festival which takes place in the palace of the Rajah of the native state where both he and Aziz are now employed....[12]

Now, having seen what the great critics say in favour of "Temple," I feel Santa Rama Rau's play shows only the tip of the Iceberg and she has failed to reveal what lies beneath the deep waters of the novel.

Her play is only *A Passage to Chandrapore*, and not—*A Passage to India.*

NOTES

1. Santa Rama Rau. *A Passage to India,* 123.
2. Malcolm Bradbury (ed.). *Forster*: *A Collection of Critical Essays* (New Delhi: PHI Private Ltd., 1979) 160-74.
3. V.A. Shahane (ed.). "Focus on Forster's: *A Passage to India,*" *Indian Essays in Criticism* (Orient Longman, 1975) 63-72.
4. Santa Rama Rau. *A Passage to India*, 126.
5. Preface books: *A Preface to Forster* by Christopher Gillie (Longman, 1983) 152.
6. Santa Rama Rau. "Recollections of E.M. Forster"/ *E.M. Forster: A Tribute,* (ed.) K. Natwar Singh (New York, 1963) 52.

7. Singh 53.
8. Santa Rama Rau. *A Passage to India,* 136.
9. V.A. Shahane (ed.). *Focus on Forster's—A Passage to India,* 122.
10. V.A. Shahane. 'Symbolism in E.M. Forster's: *A Passage to India.*' 'Temple' (*English Studies*, XLIV, Dec. 1963) 423-31.
11. Phillippa Moody. *A Critical Commentary on E.M. Forster's A Passage to India* (New York: Macmillan) 46-47.
12. Christopher Gillie. *A Preface to Forster* (Longman, 1983) 152.

WORKS CITED

Forster, E.M. *A Passage to India* (Harmondsworth: Penguin Modern Classics, 1963).

Rau, Santa Ram. *A Pasage to India.* Modern plays for students (Madras: OUP, 1978).

12

Desecration of Religious Values in *The Power and the Glory* and *Samskara:* A Comparative Study

BASAVARAJ NAIKAR

THAT THE aim of comparative study of literatures is to show the essential unity of human life is borne but by the present study of Grahman Greene's *The Power and the Glory* and U.R. Anantha Murthy's *Samskara*. Though both the texts depict two different religious contexts, yet one may see a few striking similarities between the two which help us to understand the common human tendencies all over the world.

Graham Greene's *The Power and the Glory* delineates the life of a priest against the atheistic background of Mexico whereas Anantha Murthy's *Samskara* depicts the life of a brahmin priest against an orthodox religious background. But the common theme in both the novels happens to be the desecration of religious values. As the only priest surviving in the anti-clerical Mexico, the anonymous priest is expected to uphold the high ideals of Roman Catholicism. Similarly Praneshacharya, the head-priest of Durvasapura who was educated at Kashi and has earned the title, "the Crest-Jewel of Vedanta Philosophy" is expected to uphold the ideals of Madhva brahmanism. It is on account of the moral responsibility, that these protagonists are respected by the believers of their respective faiths. The priest, though hunted by the lieutenant, representative of the Mexican Government, is looked up to by the people who are still in need of religion. Likewise Praneshacharya is respected by the brahmins of Durvasapura as a moral referee.

But the protagonists have, unfortunately, not been able to live up to the ideals expected of them. Both of them have desecrated their holy ideals, because of their weaknesses of flesh. The priest of *The Power and the Glory* has committed not only venial sins like lying, drinking, but also mortal sins like fornication. Because of his morbid alcoholism he has been nicknamed as a "whisky priest" showing the in-built contradiction. He has committed fornication with Maria in the moment of drunken loneliness and begotten an illegitimate child called Brigitta. He is aware of his sins and feels contrition. He is even mocked by his own beloved Maria as follows:

> I know you're a bad priest. That time we were together — I bet that wasn't all you've done. I've heard things, I can tell you. Do you think God wants you to stay and die—a whisky priest like you?...Suppose you die. You'll be a martyr, won't you? What kind of a martyr do you think you'll be? It's enough to make people mock (*P & G* 79).

Similarly Praneshacharya who hates Naranappa for having desecrated the brahmanical values in his life, cannot decide now whether proper brahmanical death-rite should be rendered to the dead Naranappa. Praneshacharya not only fails to take any decision about Naranappa's death-rite, but even degenerates into Naranappa's anti-brahmanical sinfulness. Naranappa who ate fish and flesh, drank liquor and slept with the low-caste Chandri had been notorious for his anti-brahmanical behaviour. But, paradoxically enough, Praneshacharya also in spite of being the Crest-Jewel of Vedanta Philosophy, stoops to the level of having sexual intercourse with Chandri. There is thus no essential difference between Naranappa, and Praneshacharya as the latter's dubious asceticism is suddenly transformed into irresistible eroticism. Hence his high idealism of brahmanism is thrown to winds. Praneshacharya enjoys the recollection of his adulterous experience with Chandri and her seductive breasts, buttocks and thighs. Adultery or fornication, thus, happens to be the common denominator of their degeneration, though the cultural contexts leading them to the sin are different. Whereas the whisky priest was compelled to indulge in fornication with Maria by his drunkenness and loneliness, Praneshacharya is tempted to have his sexual fulfilment with the low-caste Chandri when he is fully conscious of himself. The superficial brahmanical or Vedantic discipline is shattered when the floodgates of his suppressed sexual desire are opened at the slightest stimulation by Chandri in the forest at night. After having sex with Chandri, he begins to rationalise his action and even draws inspiration from Naranappa's libidinous life, Mahabala's living with a prostitute at Kashi and Shripati's regular fornication with the low-caste Belli. He even feels tempted to visit the prostitute, Padmavati at the fair. Praneshacharya, thus, becomes a symbol of sudden degeneration of brahmanical asceticism and triumph of elemental sexual instinct, or of Lawrentian dark-gods.

A difference between the whisky priest and Praneshacharya which could be noted is that whereas the fornication with Maria remains in the former as a desiccated memory, that with Chandri remains in the latter as a very lush and exciting memory.

Both the protagonists of the novels have committed many venial or minor sins in addition to the mortal or grand (*Maha papa*) sin of fornication. Whereas the whisky priest is addicted to alcoholism and gets insulted, mocked at and imprisoned for that reason, Praneshacharya commits a similar, if not the same crime, in the brahmanical context. After losing his invalid wife Praneshacharya is in a mourning period. Unable to decide about the yes or not of Naranappa's funeral, but yet under the intoxicating memory of his fornication with Chandri, Praneshacharya leaves his native village for Dharmasthala Monastery where he partakes of the community meal. Though he knows that it is wrong to desecrate the Monastery by eating the meal there when he is still mourning the death of his wife, he does so only because of his inability to control his hunger. He wants to rationalise this desecration as an emergency-ethic (*apaddharma*). In both the cases *i.e.* of the whisky priest and

Praneshacharya the desires of body triumph over those of spirit thereby showing their fall from the spiritual height.

Lying is a venial or minor sin committed by both the protagonists. The whisky priest is guilty of this sin when he tells the lieutenant that his name is Montez and the half-caste that he is not a reverend father but only a genetic father. He has this recourse to lying in order to hide his identity and escape from dangerous or embarrassing situations. Similarly Praneshacharya lies to the other brahmins of his own as well as other *agraharas* and to Putta in order to escape from their inquisitive notice.

Both the protagonists undergo an experience of metaphorical hell as a sort of punishment for their sinful behaviour. The whisky priest has a vision of hell in the prison cell where he is confined. The acrid smell of urinals and lavatory buckets, the drone of mosquitoes, shameless sexuality, criminality, agnosticism and physical discomfiture add to the whisky priest's vision of objective hell, though, of course, he feels quite comfortable in the company of other criminals. Similarly Praneshacharya also undergoes an experience of the demonic world introduced to him by Putta when the latter takes the former through the temple-festival and fair, whorehouse and pawnshop. The demonic world is full of passion and sensation like cock fighting, eating, drinking, and whoring etc. But unlike the priest who feels comfortable in the company of sinners in the dark cell, Praneshacharya does not feel totally at ease in the demonic world though he is slowly hardened enough to bear with it. Thus both the whisky priest and Praneshacharya have a temporary experience of descent into (unchristian and unbrahmanical) hell.

In both the novels, the protagonists are attacked by their opponents for their degeneration and fall from the height of ideals. The lieutenant who represents the materialistic point of view of the Mexican Government ideologically attacks the whisky priest for making a farce of the religious institution:

> 'The other,' the lieutenant said, 'is a priest.' He raised his voice: 'You know what this means — traitor to the republic. Anyone who shelters him is a traitor too? Their

> immobility seemed to anger him. He said, 'You're fools if you still believe what the priests tell you. All they want is your money. What has God ever done for you? Have you got enough to eat? Have your children got enough to eat? Instead of food they talk to you about heaven. Oh, everything will be fine after you are dead, they say. I tell you—everything will be fine when *they* are dead, and you must help' (*P & G* 74).

It is because of the hypocrisy of the religious people that the materialistic or communistic Government of Mexico is bent upon abolishing all religion and killing all the priests in the State.

Likewise Praneshacharya and his dubious brahmanism are also ideologically attacked by the inimical group of people, especially Naranappa who stands for anti-brahmanical values of life:

> 'O Acharya, who in the world can live with a girl who gives no pleasure—except of course some barren brahmins!' 'You fellows—your brahmins—you want to tie me to a hysterical female, just because she is some relative, right? Just keep your dharma to yourself—we've but one life—I belong to the "Hedonist School"—which says—barrow, if you must, but drink your ghee.'

The Acharya pleaded, 'Do whatever you want to do yourself. Please don't corrupt these boys.'

> He just laughed. 'Your Garuda, he robs shaven widows, he plots evil with black magic men, and he is one of your brahmins, isn't he?... All right, let's see who wins, Acharya. You or me? Let's see how long all this brahmin business will last. All your brahmin respectability. I'll roll it up and throw it all ways for a little bit of pleasure with one female (*Samskara* 21).

Thus in both the novels there is an ideological conflict between the religious protagonists and the irreligious antagonist. Unfortunately the protagonists are not able to live up to their own ideals because of their human weaknesses thereby rightly deserving the contempt of their enemies. In fact, they are awakened to their sins and have some kind of repentance after making a thorough search of their souls. The self-examination makes them aware of their unworthiness. The whisky priest, for example, confesses before the lieutenant in a self-analytical way:

> That other priest was right. It was when he left I began to go to pieces. One thing went after another. I got careless about my duties. I began to drink. It would have been much better, I think, if I had gone, too. Because pride was at work all the time. Not love of God.... Pride was what made the angels fall. Pride's the worst thing of all. I thought I was a fine fellow to have stayed when the others had gone. And then I thought I was so grand I could make my own rules. I gave up fasting, daily Mass. I neglected my prayers—and one day because I was drunk and lonely—well, you know how it was, I got a child (*P & G* 196).

Like the whisky priest, Praneshacharya also is aware of his weaknesses and tries to analyse his conduct retrospectively:

> I must examine unafraid even my belief that the moment occurred suddenly by itself, without my stir, in the darkness of the forest. It's true it occurred suddenly, I didn't go after it and get it. The outstretched hands touched the breasts—desire was born—there—there's the secret. That was the movement that decided which way to turn. No, a moment when I could have decided which way to turn. The answer is not that my body accepted it, but in the darkness my hands fumbled urgently, searched for Chandri's thighs and buttocks as I had never searched dharma. In that moment, decisive of which way I should turn, I took the decision to take Chandri. Even if I lost control, the responsibility to decide was still mine (*Samskara* 98).

Thus both the whisky priest and Praneshacharya have an awareness of their sins or transgressions and take the responsibility upon them. But both of them cannot change their past or even the future and are in a way ready to accept the consequences of their actions. Both of them feel a mental restlessness and undergo a psychological hell, which is almost parallel to their experience of objective hell (in the prison cell), or the demonic world (in the festival and fair).

A comparative study of the behaviour of the whisky priest and Praneshacharya, thus, reveals the common factor of their degeneration or fall from the height of ideals. The whisky priest has not been able to live up to the ideals of a Catholic saint. Similarly Praneshacharya has fallen from the brahmanical height into an anti-brahmanical level. The fall or degeneration of the two protagonists has, obviously, been caused by the weakness of flesh. Up to this point both of them are equal. But a further study of their behaviour shows that both of them are not equal, as one steals a march over the other. Comparatively speaking, the whisky priest appears to be far better than Praneshacharya because the former, in spite of being a degenerate figure, serves the purpose of his Catholic religion. In spite of being the weakest vessel, he becomes an instrument of God's cosmic design. As he confesses, "But it doesn't matter so much my being a coward—and all the rest. I can put God into a man's mouth just the same—and I can give him God's pardon. It wouldn't make any difference to that if every priest in the church was like me" (*P & G* 195). Though the whisky priest cannot rise to the level of a saint, yet he can perform the minimum duties of an ordinary priest and popularise or maintain the Catholic faith among the believers. God's love for mankind is so appalling and His glory so great that He can use even the weakest priest for the fulfilment of his providential purpose. All this makes clear that Graham Greene has an affirmative vision of life, which recognises the overall teleological beauty of the universe in spite of the occasional ugliness, which shows that even the weakest person can become an instrument of God. In Graham Greene's world, the whisky priest, in spite of his so-called fall or degeneration, can keep the institution of religion going, and in spite of his personal damnation, can help the other believers have their salvation. He, thus, serves a positive role and becomes an embodiment of the novelist's affirmative vision of life.

But Anantha Murthy's vision of life depicted in *Samskara* appears to be negative and decadent. The novelist is just contented to show the degeneration of brahmin from the dubious height of his ideals. Whereas Graham Greene shows the whisky priest struggling with an agnostic atmosphere for the continuation of religious ideals and solutions, Anantha Murthy shows a brahmin acharya coming from a religious atmosphere and yet becoming irreligious. Though the brahmin community, especially the Madhva sect has put their trust in him as a moral referee, he does not live up to their expectations by subordinating his individual physical desires to the rational control and social responsibility. By his individual fall, he brings moral disaster to the entire community, which has put an extraordinary trust in him as the Crest-Jewel of Vedanta Philosophy. Instead of solving the problem of Naranappa's death-rite for the community, he stoops to sleep with the low-caste Chandri and escapes from his village Durvasapura. He has no desire to return to his native village, and find a solution to the ethical dilemma faced by the community of Madhva brahmins. Praneshacharya, thus, becomes a symbol of fall without any suggestion of regeneration. He is more and more hardened by the non-brahmanical demonic world to accept his desecration of brahmanical values. He, thus, tries to escape from the positive world to the negative one. But the whisky priest's life strikes us to be definitely nobler than Praneshacharya's. Though the whisky priest escapes from the agnostic world of the Mexican society and Government, though he has not been the highest embodiment of Catholic ideals, yet he escapes into the religious world itself, by dying for it thereby becoming almost a martyr. He, in spite of his weaknesses, attains the nobility if not the grandeur of a martyr. Graham Greene shows his leanings towards God's party. But Praneshacharya does not show any sign of regeneration as most of his suffering is confined only to psychic level and he never undergoes the whisky priest's physical suffering like being imprisoned, being made to clean the lavatory buckets, being betrayed by the half-caste or being made to be shot dead by the Government in addition to his psychic dilemmas. Praneshacharya is more an observer than a participant, whereas the whisky priest is more a participant than an observer. Anantha Murthy seems to relish the acharya's fall and the hidden *sudra* in Naranappa and Praneshacharya.

The whisky priest, in spite of his falling short of certain ideals of his religion, enlists our sympathy by his nobility of suffering and sacrifice of his life for his faith. Thus Graham Greene's picture of a religious man's rise in spite of his fall, his death in the interest of his faith is indeed very comprehensive and conclusive, whereas Anantha Murthy's picture of Praneshacharya's life is partial and inconclusive because he does not show whether the acharya has taken any decision after the realisation of his folly and repentance. The story is left dangling at the end of *Samskara*. Anantha Murthy's philosophy appears to be negative and partial, whereas Graham Greene's is affirmative and comprehensive. That is the reason why the whisky priest's fall and rise assume the importance of an archetypal image whereas the acharya's fall remains a partial and unconvincing symbol.

Comparatively speaking, the canvas of *The Power and the Glory* is very large, as it encompasses the whole of the Mexican society and Government and the entire Catholic community, whereas that of *Samskara* is very narrow as it is confined only to the brahmin, especially Madhva brahmin community having minor bickering with other sub-sects like Smartas and the liberal brahmins of Kundapura. *The Power and the Glory* thus concerns itself with the large entities geographically, politically and religiously, whereas *Samskara* is limited to small entities of life geographically (confined only to Durvasapura, Kundapura and in between villages) and religiously (confined only to sectarian brahmins' dilemmas).

The plot of *The Power and the Glory* is double dimensional in that it can be read both as a thriller on a secular level and as a religious novel. It appeals both to the non-Catholic reader and to the Catholic one. The materialistic triumph of the Mexican Government in hunting out the last priest and killing him by way of punishment also involves the concurrent sacrifice of the priest for his faith or ideal. Thus both the lieutenant (representative of the communist Government) and the whisky priest are triumphant in their own ways. Whereas the Government (State) triumphs over the priest (Church), the priest becomes triumphant by laying down his life for his faith. This kind of double-dimensionality cannot be found in *Samskara* which shows only the triumph of flesh over spirit, instinct over reason, *sudra* tendency over brahmanism, and, therefore, operates only on one dimension.

Both the novels contain some symbolic motifs. Whereas eagles in *The Power and the Glory* symbolise evil and death, vultures in *Samskara* symbolise death and decadent brahmanism. Likewise mosquitoes and malaria hold a mirror to the physical disease and symbolise moral corruption in Mexico, rats and plague reflect the deadliness of the disease and fast rate of morality in the villages around Durvasapura. In both the novels, physical disease complements the moral decadence. Anantha Murthy's description of rats and people dying on account of being inflicted by plague seems to be relatively overdone as he appears to be overtly influenced by Albert Camus' *The Plague.*

One is easily struck by the difference of style in both the novels. The general impression created on the mind of the reader happens to be that the language of *Samskara* appears to be more poetic and picturesque than that of *The Power and the Glory* which is relatively dry and denotes dehydration of emotion which is, perhaps, due to Graham Greene's early training in film-script writing.

Both the novels are based upon actual events that happened in life some time ago. As Graham Greene has mentioned somewhere, his whisky priest was partially based upon the life of a hunted priest in Mexico. Similarly Anantha Murthy has confessed in the Kannada journal *Rujuvatu* that though his Praneshacharya was based upon a real brahmin of south India, he was inspired to write such a novel only after seeing a Russian film in Birmingham.

The comparative study of the two novels has shown us the

emergence of a universal pattern *i.e.* desecration of religious values, in spite of cultural dissimilarities and particularities.

NOTE

All the references to the texts are from (1) *The Power and the Glory*, by Graham Greene, Harmondsworth: Penguin Books, 1970. Cited as *P & G*. (2) *Samskara*, by U.R. Anantha Murthy, Translated by A.K. Ramanujan (Delhi, OUP, 1985).

13

Treatment of Evil in Steinbeck's *The Pearl* and Chaucer's *The Pardoner's Tale*

M.A. NARE

LET ME at the outset say that in this brief critical paper I would like to examine the treatment of Evil in the novels *The Pearl* and *The Pardoner's Tale*.

In *The Pearl*, Evil is introduced as a poisonous scorpion that stings Kino's innocent baby (a son) Coyotito. This dramatic incident in the novel prepares our minds to understand how Evil is going to invade peace and harmony in the life of a happy couple—Kino and Juana. Juana is an ideal wife. She inherits all folk wisdom. She asks her husband to call the doctor to treat their only son—Coyotito. They know he won't come. For, the doctor looked down upon the natives—the Indians. They are poor people. He is from Spain.

They go to his place but he refuses to see them.

"Have I nothing better to do than cure insect bites for 'the little Indians? (315). I am a doctor not a veterinary." They waited at the gate. At last, Kino "struck the gate a crushing blow with his fist. He looked down in wonder at his split knuckles, at the blood" (316).

From this symbolic action we find how the suppressed anger against the doctor's race wants to erupt like a volcano. This racial hatred plays a great part in the events to come.

Kino's people were exploited for four hundred years. He can't forget that. He wants his child to live. Juana's knowledge of herbal medicine saves the child.

Then he finds a pearl "as large as a sea-gull's egg." It is the greatest pearl in the world. The whole town begins to vibrate with this great incident in poor Kino's life.

Now, Kino's ambition grows. He wants to marry in the church, he wants to buy a rifle, and he wants to educate his son.

But Kino knows—

> "also that the gods do not love success unless it comes by accident. He knew that the gods take their revenge on man if he be successful through his own efforts" (337).

Now, the doctor comes to know of the Great Pearl. He is a wicked man. He wants to trap Kino to grab his pearl. Kino does not trust him. The doctor sends his men to steal the pearl in the night. But Kino was alert. He jumped like an angry cat with his knife and tried to grab the shadowy thing but it escaped.

From this moment Juana tries to save him from "cold and brooding hate."

"This thing is evil," she cried harshly. "This pearl is like sin! It will destroy us," and her voice rose shrilly. "Throw it away Kino. Let us break it between stones. Let us bury it and forget the place. Let us throw it back into the sea. It has brought evil. Kino, my husband, it will destroy us."

* * *

"This is our one chance," our son must go to school. He must break out of the pot that holds us in" (349). "It will destroy us all," Juana cried, "Even our son." But he does not care for her warnings—now he is a blind man walking towards a precipice. His fall is inevitable.

He was so happy with his pearl.

"So lovely it was, so soft and its own music came from it—its music of promise and delight, its guarantee of the future, of comfort, of security. Its warm lucency promised a poultice against illness and a wall against insult. It closed a door on hunger..." (350).

Juana was helpless, she had to obey him. "He was a man"—and she wanted him.

The pearl-buyers in the town try to deceive him. They say, "it's like fool's gold." It is not a pearl, it is a monstrosity.

Kino wants to go to the city to sell it. His brother has his own fears because "he has defied the whole structure." Juan Thomas embraced his brother with the double embrace and kissed him on both cheeks. "Go with God," he said, and it was like death. "You will not give up the pearl?"

* * *

"This pearl has become my soul," said Kino. "If I give it up I shall lose my soul. Go thou also with God." These words show how the evil has taken possession of his soul.

Juana tries to throw away that pearl but Kino snatches the pearl from her, and kicks her like a brute. Then he kills a man who tries to attack him. But he confesses his guilt before his wife and before his brother.

Then they escape secretly from the town.

But Kino knows he would be chased by the trackers. He goes to the rocky mountains and asks his wife to rest in a small cave and like a guard he observes vigilantly the movements of the three trackers.

And when they approach near the cave he kills them mercilessly. "And then Kino's brain cleared from its red concentration and he knew the sound—the keening, moaning, rising hysterical cry from the little cave in the side of the stone mountain, the cry of death" (409).

He goes back to the cave and finds Coyotito lying in the little cave with the top of his head shot away.

They return home. They pass through their town La Paz as strangers.

"Their eyes glanced neither right nor left nor up nor down but stared only straight ahead. Their legs moved little jerkily, like well-made wooden dolls, and they carried pillars of black fear about them" (410). They go to the sea. Kino sits there, puts down his rifle and wants to look at the pearl. "The pearl was ugly, it was gray like a malignant growth. And Kino heard the music of the pearl distorted and insane" (412).

Juana stood beside him holding her dead bundle over her shoulder.

And then Kino flung the pearl with all his might. Then the music of the pearl gradually disappeared.

In fact, in losing the pearl he has found his soul—a way to his salvation is cleared.

This tragic story of a simple diver works on various levels.

- It is an allegory or a parable.
- It has a great symbolic structure.
- It narrates the fall of Kino and also his "rebirth."
- Kino is an Everyman.

According to Buddhist Doctrine Kino can attain his salvation through a series of "rebirths." The story does not end like *The Pardoner's Tale, Dr. Faustus* or *Macbeth.* The Christian impact seems very thin in this tale. Buddha's Doctrine shows how evil works on human mind:

> There is no such thing as positive or absolute evil. Everything temporal is relative, including things morally good or bad. Both expressions denote merely the higher or lower degree of egotism of a living being, whose roots are the will-to-live and ignorance. No living being, no matter how deeply it may be sunk in selfishness and ignorance is excluded from the possibility of emancipation, of salvation. Everyone can attain wisdom and perfection, *if he really strives for them*, though perhaps only through a long series of rebirths.[1]

In this tale Kino passes through various stages of sufferings because of this ignorance (illusion or Maya) and his will-to-live (Tanha□). But in the end we find how he was changed. When Kino threw back the pearl to the sea, he regained his soul. He has undergone a kind of rebirth like the Ancient Mariner.

The Buddhist philosophy must be at the back of Steinbeck's mind when he composed this tale. The story has crossed the Christian frame—it has broadened its spiritual horizon.

Dr. S.T. Kallapur's article, "John Steinbeck and Oriental Thought: Some Parallels" shows, "A careful reading of his books provides the reader with some internal evidence of Steinbeck's knowledge of Indian books." Here he gives a list of books and item (vi) clearly shows "some book(s) on Gautama Buddha, his life and his philosophy." He further writes:

> However, it is clear, that many of Steinbeck's important conceptions are more Hinduistic than Christian, more Eastern than Western.[2]

The end of *The Pearl* fits in the Buddhist framework rather than the Christian one. The Christian hero like Dr. Faustus must perish—must be damned. There is no hope of salvation for him.

The Pardoner's Tale by Chaucer is used as a sermon on Greed by a Christian Pardoner who himself is greedy. The Medieval Church used to frighten its followers with the pictures of Death or Devils. By introducing the fear of the Devil, they tried to exploit them.

The Pardoner's Tale also has its roots in *The Jataka Tales* of Buddha. These tales travelled with sailors to European countries and were used for sermons by Christian fathers. The wise old man in this tale looks like a Buddhist Monk. There is a reference to India. His behaviour shows he has understood the evil power of a heap of gold florins. He was running away like a frightened man. He was afraid of the Evil power of gold.

But the foolish young men want to find out Death. They want to kill Death.

"Where Angels fear to tread fools rush in." The foolish, young gamblers go to the oak tree to find a heap of gold florins. The moment they saw that great heap they forgot their vows, their co-called bond of brotherhood. Greed for gold kills them.

The story shows that the root cause of their death is lack of wisdom which the old man possessed in abundance. When they die, we are not shocked, we don't suffer with them. For they are not like us.

While Kino is like us. We suffer with him. We have sympathy for him. We are happy when he finally throws away that evil pearl.

Kino is an Everyman.

If we take the Christian parable of the Pearl then the savage in Kino throws away the Pearl, the symbol of salvation. Then he will be an Anti-Everyman.

The story *The Pearl* has a complex design. It works on various levels.

The Buddhist impact on it is so obvious that the right kind of interpretation of the story is possible only when we accept the Buddhist Doctrine of Salvation.

But we must admit that both the currents—Christian as well as Buddhist—mix and mingle in this complex work of art.

Chaucer's *Pardoner's Tale* uses Evil only to frighten the foolish sinners. The sinners are punished by God.

In *The Pearl* this simple formula does not work. The last scene suggests that Kino has undergone, through the agony of his soul, a sort of "re-birth."

Now, he has "the sea" before him to wash his sins. We feel he will seek his salvation like the ancient mariner.

REFERENCES

1. Bhikku, Subhadra. *The Message of Buddhism.* Ed. by J.E. Ellam (London: Kegan Paul Trench, Trubner & Co. Ltd., 1922) 64.
2. Sharma, R.K. (ed.). *Indian Response to Steinbeck* (Jaipur: Rachana Prakashan, 1984) 17.

NOTE

Noble's Comparative Classics: *Silas Marner—The Pearl* edited by Jay E. Green. (New York: Noble and Noble, 1965). The page nos. in parentheses are from this edition of *The Pearl.*

14

Women Protagonists in Wharton and Sivasankari: A Feminist Perspective

STELLA

BEING THE world's foremost democracy, America seems to stand for the goal of freedom for all her citizens, freedom being the first of America's professed, tripartite values of liberty, equality and fraternity, expatiated and propagated by thinkers like Emerson, Thoreau and Whitman. Emerson advocates the cause of individualism in *The American Scholar* thus:

> The world is nothing, the man is all; in yourself is the law of all nature...in yourself slumbers the whole of Reason. Nation of men will for the first time exist, because each believes himself inspired by the Divine/Soul (1837: 60).

In "Wharton Questions Motherhood" Kaiku Bappu finds Wharton far ahead of her time in questioning the "Myth of motherhood" that on the one hand, glorifies mothers as sacred, and on the other, subjugates them to the ideal of maternity and produces frustrated, repressed, disturbed and martyred women. In *The Children* and *The Mother's Recompense*, says Bappu, Wharton criticised both the traditional and modern motherhood with an incisive insight.

Annis Pratt's *Archetypal Patterns in Women's Fiction* too highlights the historic iconoclastic role played by the women artists, in the history of women's emancipation: "Women writers dig up the goddess from the ruins, clean the debris from the face, casting aside the gynophobic masks that obscured her beauty, her power and her beneficence" (178).

Edith Wharton belongs to such a group of novelists who are passionately concerned with the emancipation of women. Perhaps it is appropriate in this context, to bring in the Ardener's diagram, concerning the boundaries of the spheres of interest:

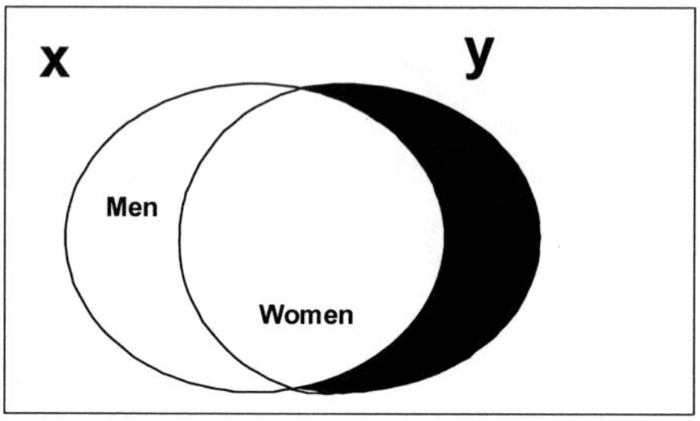

Diagram

In the above diagram, x and y stand for the boundaries of the spheres of interest of men and women respectively. Ardener projects as if much of "y" falls within the boundaries of "x" when the spheres intersect each other. That which is outside the dominant boundary is, in Ardener's terminology, "wild." Seema Jene tells us how Ardener and critics like Elaine Showalter have agreed "that women's writing is not inside or outside the male tradition, but inside the two traditions simultaneously" (19), the two being complementary to each other.

In fact, Wharton had no particularly sentimental devotion to her own native place and did not care much for Newport, as her husband did. As for her convention-bound community around, Kellogg tells us how "its social functions bored her...she kept busy with her little house. One may surmise that her neighbour sensed and somewhat resented her independence" (72).

Edith Wharton is much obsessed with the theme of the independence of women, to which she gives eloquent expression in most of her works. It seems quite possible that Wharton's pronounced defiant posture towards a male-dominated society, was occasioned by her own early experiences as a young woman. In a typically democratic situation, an individual's liberty is almost dependent on the other equally valid principles of equality and fraternity. Lack of any one of these three fundamental principles will ultimately end up in a chaos of values.

For instance, Bessy in *The Fruit of the Tree* turns out to be a daring rebel, despite all the unreasonable financial restrictions laid down by her husband. Bessy's happiness over marrying Amherst, the man of her choice, vanishes the moment her economic independence, and consequently, her personal independence get curbed in several ways by Amherst. While Bessy continues to indulge herself in luxuries like "a set of Chinese vases for twenty-five hundred dollars...and a pair of cobs" (287) as was her vogue before marriage, Amherst proves himself to be "a calculating brute who has married her for her fortune" (324). He also raises objections to Bessy's needless purchase of a horse, when a steamer is already available for her. However, Bessy's contention is, "with only one motor, one must have more horses, of course" (287).

In sharp contrast to Amherst's meanness, Bessy gives him a free hand to spend her money towards the fulfilment of his plans at Westmore. On one occasion, she tells him, "I always expected that you would need a great deal more money than you thought...(286). These words clearly demonstrate Bessy's extraordinary generosity of spirit and understanding of her husband. It is little wonder then that Bessy has every reason to resent Amherst's persistent attempts to restrict her spending. She feels highly annoyed when he observes: "Your expenses will have to be cut down a great deal...they are increasing steadily" (287). Essentially, deep within herself, Amherst's interest in Westmore, "his safety valve, his refuge" is of no importance to Bessy. If only she had had her way, she feels she would not have begun, "this horrible house" (at Westmore) (36). Once, she expresses her discontentment to Justine, who in turn, confides it to Amherst that "Bessy has not been quite content of late to give you so much time to Westmore...because Westmore takes you from her" (253). Even more important, Bessy is denied the opportunity of indulging herself with her own daughter.

Bessy's personal happiness is lost not only because of

Amherst's commitment to Westmore but also because of his indifference towards her daughter, Cecily. On one occasion, Wharton comments how Bessy "alternated between moments of exaggerated devotion and days of neglect, never for long happy, away from the girl" (259). At one point she begins to feel guilty of being extremely selfish as a wife and "of sacrificing her child's prospects to further Amherst's enterprise and therefore she dashes...upstairs [to]...do penance beside her child's bed" (262). Moreover, Amherst disapproves of Bessy's horse-riding, while Bessy "shows a great zeal in the pursuit of sport—a tireless passion for the saddle, the golf-course, the tennis-court, with an almost Oriental inertia within doors" (219). Amherst who does not understand this absorbing passion in his energetic wife, frustrates Bessy through a letter addressed to Justine, Bessy's nurse, with a simple injunction: "don't let my wife ride Impulse" (372). Amherst also objects to Bessy's intimacy with the Carburys, but in this regard Bessy dares to disobey him, as she finds him totally unreasonable. Bessy's rebellion can be seen from the butler's cryptic reports to Amherst: "Mrs. Amherst has gone away...this afternoon, Sir, to Mapleside...by motor...to stay with Mrs. Carbury (341). Once, referring to the Carburys, Bessy's mother charges Amherst with the words: "you have my daughter cut off from all her friends" (216). Though the Carburys are addicted to playing bridge for money, Bessy herself does not do so. All these acts of nonconformity on the part of Bessy, are sure signs of incipient rebellion simmering deep within her, which do not go totally unnoticed. Bessy too begins to openly retort "to his assertion of independence" (345). Consequently, Amherst refuses permission to Bessy even for a few weeks' rest in Europe, which could have revived her health and vitality.

Amherst who feels inwardly more pleased with the arrangement, says to Justine, "her little excursion with you did her well...I think she only needed rest. Perhaps her six weeks in the Adrion docks were better than Europe" (210). But Amherst's assessment of the situation proves to be utterly absurd, as owing to his continued negligence, Bessy's health has already begun to deteriorate, and she is thoroughly "unhappy" (197) and proves to be "so wasteful of her strength of nerves" (210). Even more important, Bessy not only loses faith in herself as an individual, but suddenly realises with a sense of terror that women can have no faith "in their own ability to change their environment because they have been taught that women cannot make it through life—economically, socially, emotionally or sexually without men" (134).

Bessy is later completely cured of her illusions, caused by her blind love for Amherst, as she realises that she is "no more to him than the carpet on the floor" (230). She who had been all along so flexible and thus "the dearest little Chameleon" (160), learns gradually that "every woman must fight her battles alone." As "her love for Amherst was dead" (413), she initiates an open debate with him saying, "Is that what you marry for?" (236).

Louis Auchincloss's assessment looks rather naïve when she comments, "although twenty-four years old, widowed and a mother by that time...she is in short, both ignorant and spoiled" (52). Even Blake Nevius' observation: "Bessy is a composite portrait of everything that Edith Wharton disliked in her own sex" (104) seems to be considerably prejudiced. On the contrary, Bessy emerges through all her ordeals as triumphant fighter, who does not give in till the very end. In the will "made some months before her death," "Bessy had divided her estate between her husband and her daughter, placing Cecily's share in trust," (436) and her final shrewd move comes as a nasty surprise to Amherst. All her favourite projects like the pleasure-house, gymnasium and hospital are implemented now in complete accordance with her desire:

> The Emergency Hospital, planned in the first months of his marriage and abandoned in the general reduction of expenditure at the mills, had now been completed on a larger and more elaborate scale, as a memorial to Bessy (439).

Bessy's project at Lynbrook is eventually carried out in letter and spirit by Amherst himself, in the end. Even at the cost of her own economic and personal independence, Bessy ensures her daughter's freedom. Her property is duly passed on to Cecily, as per the provisions in her will, and is eventually shared by the labourers, for Cecily herself declares, "In my mother's name, I give this house to Westmore" (629). Now, everyone can see the profound influence exercised by Bessy on her daughter and "the impetus of self-sacrifice had carried her straight to her good" (557). Further, once liberty is attained, equality and fraternity are concomittantly also assured, as symbolically presented in the novel through the union of Justine Brent, Bessy's nurse, with Amherst, who has now become Bessy's equal through marriage.

In Wharton's *The House of Mirth*, it is Lily who rebels against tradition and the established moral code of conduct from the beginning. She takes to smoking cigarettes in public quite early and wears fashionable dresses of her choice. Judy openly warns her against such exhibitionism: "Don't wear your scarlet '*cripe de chine*' for dinner and don't smoke" (47). Percy Gryce is shocked at her addiction to the game of bridge for "he had never seen a girl play cards for money" (81). As for Lily, the game is simply irresistible for "the gambling passion was upon her" (28).

Being a born fighter for freedom, Lily detests dependence of all kinds. What she actually yearns for is "freedom from everything—from money, from poverty, from ease and anxiety, from all the material accidents" (71). Whenever Lily says, "she is free and I am not" (7), what she puts her finger on is her frustration over her own economic dependence on Mrs. Peniston, her aunt and guardian: "She was beginning to chafe at the obligations...to feel herself a mere pensioner of the splendour which had once seemed to belong to her" (27). She yields to the temptation of playing bridge only with the intention of winning a large sum of money through a windfall now and then, to just lavish on trinkets and dresses, for after all, "Once or twice she had won a large sum…" (28). Lily thinks independently and acts impulsively though her happiness is often marred by her fear of her aunt, who admonishes her from time to time, and also her fear of the hypocritical society around. To Lily, the mere act of living in society is to follow a stratagem, "to calculate and contrive and retreat and advance as if...going through an intricate dance, where one misstep would throw...hopelessly out of tune" (49-50). Lily is also ambitious and quite fastidious, with regard to her collection of diamond jewellery and it is this weakness in character that drives her, subsequently, to risk higher stakes with each of her fresh ventures. She feels at first, quite impatient with her position of not having a motorcar or a steam-yacht at her orders, "but the daily friction of unpaid bills, the daily nibble of small temptations to expenditure were trials as far out of her experience as the domestic problems of the charwoman" (80). It is only with a view to asserting her independence from her aunt, Mrs. Peniston, that Lily seeks the help of Augustus Trenor, who deals with "tips" and "deals."

Lily also fights in defence of her personal dignity and independence with regard to all her relationships. When men like Percy Gryce, Simon Rosedale and Selden make offers of marriage to her, in relation to the degree of the wealth each of them has at his command, Lily coolly rejects all of them one by one. "She is discerning enough to know" (22) the ulterior design of men in general and of Augustus Trenor in particular. Moreover, she is always on the alert to escape from being entangled in the enticing web of men.

Lily's determination to preserve her personal honour, goads her on to work hard, in order to pay off the debt she owes Augustus Trenor and, consequently, she dies happily, pleased with all her efforts. To start with, her ultimate purpose in life seems to be to make the most of life, her watchword being, "I like being happy" (7). She is also over-conscious of her external appearance. But in her mature phase Lily is even prepared to work as Mrs. Hatch's secretary, a job she had looked upon with contempt earlier. She has become humble enough to say: "She (Mrs. Hatch) has helped me to earn a living when my old friends were quite resigned to seeing me starve" (294). She also works as a milliner's apprentice at St Regina's, all with a view to saving her honour. She confesses the gross error she had committed to Mrs. Hatch on one occasion: "Unfortunately, I had spent the money (9000 dollars) before I discovered my mistake—that's why I am trying to learn a trade" (307). She realises only too well "the value of money" and prefers an honourable hand-to-mouth existence to a dishonourable life of affluence. This trait of resisting the charms of wealth itself marks her lately-attained maturity and strength of character. Though she has not a penny left after paying off Gus Trenor's debt of ten thousand dollars, she wins a meritorious moral battle in the end.

Ironically, Lily, a born aristocrat, dies as a working class woman. Yet her character reveals an admirable spirit of defiance against all the false values of the world. The equality she aspires for with the poor at the time of her death is symbolically conveyed in the novel, through her holding a baby of the working class in her hands:

> The baby feeling herself detached from her habitual anchorage made an instructive motion of resistance...Lily felt the soft weight sink trustfully against her breast.... At first the burden in her arms seemed as light as a pink cloud or a heap of down, but as she continued to hold it, the weight increased, sinking deeper—as though the child entered into her and became a part of herself (333).

The yawning gulf between the aristocracy and the proletariat has thus been bridged by Lily's death.

Wharton's nineteenth-century stance in relation to the tenets of feminism in America is akin to Sivasankari's attitude towards women of the twentieth-century India. Sivasankari too feels it her responsibility as a writer to bring out in the open the suppressed feelings of women over the centuries, echoing the words of Margaret Mead: "The emotional part of women's life—that part which makes her a woman must be brought out of the dark and allowed to put forth its best" (147).

Sivasankari's independence of mind is reflected in almost all her women protagonists recalling the following lines of Michael Judith and Ann Orkleyed: "A woman must have sense and independence of mind...meek wives are foolish mothers" (128-29). As a writer Sivasankari discusses with a candour, ability and sincerity, the various struggles put up by women in India to gain greater independence for themselves. In the words of Susie Tharu and Lalitha, "The new woman was self-confident, autonomous and this was a figure that was to dominate the literary imagination for several decades to come" (*WWI* 173).

Visali in *47 Natkal* is grossly misjudged as gullible and treated little better than a fool, who can be easily carried away by attractive presents like sarees and watches by Kumar, her wicked husband. Visali rightly smells that there is something fishy when Kumar disappears on the nuptial-night itself. The incident shows that Visali, though illiterate is not ignorant. Once her suspicion proves to be true, Kumar openly announces that Lucia is actually his first wife. To Kumar's shock the tradition-bound Visali succeeds in breaking the mask of thraldom in her marriage with a cheat. She strives hard to overcome the depression that often goads her on, right to the verge of committing suicide. Therefore, she hits upon a plan to escape the clutches of Kumar, either through Lucia by showing her the wedlock or by meeting one of the Indian families she is likely to come across, on her way to shopping.

Visali preserves her will intact, even when Kumar ill-treats her, going to the extent of burning one of her fingers once. She turns a deaf ear to all his harsh words, thus paving the way for still greater utterly unexpected consequences. Her love for Kumar has now turned to bitter hatred, and she tells him to his face: "how I hate you touching me" (161). Kumar has become more and more rude towards her. Visali decides now to give him up, even though she will be helpless living in a foreign land, and having to use a foreign language. However, she avails of the first opportunity that comes her way and expresses her predicament to one of the Indian families, using the only word in English "help," which she has picked up from an English movie and shows all possible gestures to make them understand the seriousness of her situation. Visali's daring efforts prove eventually fruitful. One Mr. Dharunkurmar sees the ambassador on her behalf and informs him of Visali's plight, who in turn puts up a trunk-call to a minister and with much difficulty, they all succeed in tracing her brother and Visali finds security at last in her brother's home.

Visali daringly and unexpectedly, severs not only the sentimental attachment of a wife to her husband but also of a mother to her child. She throws away the wedlock that has so long bound her to a blind, unquestioned tradition and aborts her foetus with Lucia's aid, as she feels it a sin to carry his child in her womb. She even asks once "How much would I have sinned to carry his child in my womb?" (206). Thus not only does Visali escape from her doomed fate but succeeds in sealing Kumar's fate too. She shatters his world of illusions by making him realise her true worth, and by encouraging Lucia also to leave him for ever. Now she returns home at last, relieved after a frantic period of forty-seven days.

Chandra in *Mukkanankayiru* lays a fitting snare for Moorthy and takes the initiative in deciding his fate. Indeed, it is Mano, her son who opens her eyes to her blind acceptance of all her sufferings in life in the name of fate, for the sake of her children. She decides at last: "I should make the right decision right now. I cannot afford to remain the same old Chandra, enduring everything forever" (45). However, it is too late when she realises the need for such a change in her attitude towards Moorthy. Initiating a probe, she finds out that Moorthy very often takes out Nalini, his colleague in the office, either on official or unofficial grounds. She is furious at the words of Nalini's father, who tells her in a heartless fashion: "You do not give Moorthy any peace at home. His condition has become pathetic. At least he finds a little comfort in Nalini's companionship. Should you destroy even that? Are you really a woman?" (56).

Chandra daringly faces such odds, each time rising to the occasion. Once, she realises the meaninglessness of continuing her miserable married life, with a sensitive, adolescent son like Mano, who keeps complaining to her whenever he catches his father on the wrong foot: "Yesterday I saw daddy in the company of Nalini" (24); "I myself saw him fully drunk, blabbering and with four or five women" (32). Cut to the quick at last, Chandra gives her consent to Moorthy, to marry Nalini and takes a fervent interest in making all the preliminary arrangements for the consummation of their marriage. Initially, she wins their admiration with her seemingly apologetic and confessional tone, accepting that only now she has realised her mistake of not satisfying her husband's wishes so far. It is only at the end that she reveals her real intention when, once again, Moorthy slowly makes advances to her:

> The wedlock that Nalini is wearing now around her neck, is the noose strung through your nose, as even as an uncontrollable heifer is brought under control by the noose piercing through the holes of its nostrils. This marriage is sure to turn a life sentence for you (105).

From now on, Moorthy ceases to be her husband. She knows it is meaningless to live with him, for there is "no kindness in his glance, concern in his words or grace in his conduct; absolutely none" (6-7).

In Edith Wharton, all her protagonists, with the exception of Bessy, are "new women" in their values and behaviour. It is exclusively their own responsibility to solve their problems. Though Bessy is excluded from this list, in a way, she too triumphs over her obstacles, in her own quiet way. Wharton's women are confident that they can contravene every wily, chauvinistic move on the part of their men.

In Sivasankari's world of fiction, most of her heroines, are quite conventional to start with, and they gradually evolve into "new women." Mohana, the ex-call-girl of Delhi, being the only exception. The only married woman, who evolves into a "new woman" is the childless Lavanya. All the protagonists ultimately manage to find their way out to freedom from the clutches of heartless, materialistic and chauvinistic men in their lives.

WORK CITED

Auchincloss, Louis. *Edith Wharton: A Woman in her Time* (New York: Viking Press, 1911).

Nevius, Blake. *Edith Wharton: A Study of her fiction* (Berkeley & Los Angeles: University of California Press, 1953).

Pratt, Annis. *Archetypal Patterns in Woman's Fiction* (Bloomington: Indiana UP, 1981).

Sivasankari. *47 Natkal* (Chennai: Vanati Publishers, 1978).

——. *Mukkanankayiru* (Chennai: Tirumakal Nilayam, 1982).

Tharu, Susie and Lailitha K. (ed.). *Women's Writing in India 600 B.C. to the Present* (New York: The Feminist Press, 1991). Cited as *WWI.*

Wharton, Edith. *The House of Mirth* (1905, rpt. New York: Macmillan, 1907).

——. *The Fruit of the Tree* (1907, rpt. New York: Virago, 1988).

15

A Comparative Study of Mamta Kalia's Poem: "Tribute to Papa" and Sylvia Plath's "Daddy"

VEENA NARE

IN THIS brief paper, I would like to examine Mamta Kalia's poem: "Tribute to Papa" and compare it with Sylvia Plath's "Daddy."

I would like to show how Mamta Kalia in her poem presents a modern sensibility while Sylvia Plath through her poem "Daddy" presents the extreme end of attachment through the "girl's Electra complex for her father."

Mamta's attitude towards her father no doubt reveals the impact of modern Indian life on her psyche but at the same time it is somewhat—astonishing in the Indian context. She appears to be bold in her speech but on the other hand seems to defend the corrupt world around when she says:

> Who cares for you Papa?
> Who cares for your clean thoughts, clean
> words, clean teeth?
> Who wants to be an angel like you?
> Who wants it.

She appears frustrated and makes a desperate attempt on her part to adjust with the world around. Her frustration gives her a feeling that her father has been an "unsuccessfulman" as his dreams were limited and so couldn't secure a "cosy" place in this world. She even goes to the extent of saying:

> I wish you had guts Papa,

To smuggle eighty thousand watches at a
stroke,
And I'd proudly say, 'My father's in
Import-export business, you know.'
I'd be proud of you then.

Poetry is a criticism of life and it is revealed through the above lines. Mamta is attached to her father but in this world of "easy money" the definition of value has changed. His ideal life and his efforts to be a role model give her a feeling of suffocation. She mocks at his prayers when she says:

When you can't think of doing anything,
You start praying,
Spending useless hours at the temple.

The struggle in Mamta's mind appears to be superficial. The poem also reveals her personality, which finds the new world more tantalising. Her feminist view is revealed when she further says:

I give two donkey-claps for your greatness.
And three for Rani Lakshmibai.
These days I am seriously thinking of
disowning you, Papa
You and your sacredness.

These lines reveal the two faces of Mamta. She is able to detach herself from her father easily and feminism takes a back seat when she says:

Everything about you clashes with nearly
everything about me.

The following lines:

You suspect I am having a love affair
these days,
But you're too shy to have it confirmed.
What if my tummy starts growing gradually
And I refuse to have it curetted?
But I'll be careful Papa,
Or I know you'll at once think of suicide.

reveal the fear of her "Papa" as he suspects that the daughter is having a love affair and can give birth to a child before marriage. Mamta's fear makes her to say, "I'll be careful Papa" otherwise she feels he may commit suicide. This I feel is a mask that Mamta wears, as she knows that her father would not commit suicide.

The Indian social life and culture restrict her in her attempt to be free from the bondages of values represented by her father. Mamta's "Papa" is a simple, honest and a religious man who according to her is a misfit in this society.

In "Daddy," Sylvia Plath is very personal and true in her rendering of the experiences. She was deeply attached to her father and loved him like God. Sylvia felt trapped in her love for her father for nearly thirty years.

The opening lines of the poem:

> You do not do, you do not do
> Any more, black shoe
> In which I have lived like a foot
> For thirty years, poor and white,
> Barely daring to breathe or Achoo.

reveal the Electra complex which Sylvia Plath suffered in her life. She lived under the influence of her father who was a careless German. He was a diabetic who neglected the injury on his toe, which resulted in amputation and his sudden death. It was a great blow to the young child Sylvia, who was "ten when they buried him."

The second stanza throws light on this personal experience:

> Daddy, I have had to kill you.
> You died before I had time—
> Marble—heavy, a bag full of God,
> Ghostly statue with one grey toe
> Big as a frisco seal

Sylvia's "Daddy" was a Nazi while her mother was a Jew. This internal conflict creates a psychological tension, which is reflected through the following lines:

> So I never could tell where you
> Put your foot, your root,
> I never could talk to you.

The lines:

I thought every German was you.
And the language obscene

An engine, An engine
Chuffing me off like a Jew
A Jew to Dachau, Auschwitz, Belsen.
I began to talk like a Jew.
I think I may well be a Jew.

intensify her conflict and make the experience more real and true.

Plath is afraid of the powerful Nazi image of her father which is reflected through the words "neat moustache," "Aryan eye," "Panzer-man" and the symbol of the Nazi's: Swastika—which is not a religious symbol but a political one.

Sylvia has a desire to kill her father and thus the God like image changes into the devil image when she talks about his picture, which shows the "cleft in his chin instead of his foot." She refers to her father as "no less a devil" and a "black man" "who bit her pretty red heart into two."

Even after the death of her father, Sylvia had a strong urge to be with him and hence attempted suicide on 24th August 1953 at the age of twenty. The lines:

At twenty I tried to die
And get back, back, back to you
I thought even the bones would do.

express the father fixation as a great crisis in her life.

She survived this attempt and married Ted Hughes, the English poet in whom she saw her father. She felt relieved after the marriage as she succeeded in killing her father through the marriage. But the crisis in marriage separated her from her husband, after seven years of their married life. This resulted in killing the father image in her husband as well and made her to say:

If I've killed one man, I've killed two—
The vampire who said he was you
And drank my blood for a year.

Seven years, if you want to know.
Daddy, you can lie back now.

These images reveal the feminist view of Sylvia, which was not adopted, but was very personal. The crisis in her life finally led her to commit suicide on 11th February 1963.

Just as D.H. Lawrence's novel *Sons and Lovers* is a personal experience of the author's Oedipus complex, Sylvia Plath's "Daddy" fits perfectly into the Freudian concept of Electra complex.

The real suffering in Sylvia's life has made the poem very powerful. Mamta has used her "Papa" as a symbol of old traditions and values. The change in the society becomes the central theme of Mamta's poem.

Thus "Tribute to Papa" appears to be a kind of mask Mamta wore to portray the social life.

While Sylvia's "Daddy" is more truthful as it portrays the real suffering in her life right from childhood to the date of composition of her poem.

WORKS CITED

Deshpande, Gauri (ed.). *An Anthology of Indian English Poetry*, An Orient Paperback.

Salunke, Vilas (ed.). *The Mystic Drum: An Anthology of Poems in English* (Pune: Poona University, 1999).

16

Browning and Tagore: Their Poems on Religious Thoughts

JAYANTA BHATTACHARYA

IT IS quite interesting to note that both Browning and Tagore were brought up at home wherein prevailed a religious atmosphere. Browning's mother inherited the German and Scotch traditions and this created in Browning a metaphysical tendency. His mother was a pious lady, and in the way of training she imparted religious teaching to Browning. And in the case of Rabindranath the strong religious influence came from his father Debendranath Tagore who hated all idolatry, and gave a new interpretation of Hinduism. Undoubtedly, Rabindranath's theism largely incorporated his father's religious convictions. Both poets afterwards systematically developed their concepts of God and His creations—the universe, nature, man and all other forms of life, etc.

In Browning, Paracelsus has a grand vision which echoes Goethean idea:

> Thus [God] dwells in all,
> From life's minute beginnings, up at last
> To Man—the consummation of this Scheme
> Of Being—the completion of this sphere
> Of Life, whose attributes had here and there
> Been scattered o'er the visible world before,
> Asking to be combined...dim fragments meant
> To be united in some wondrous whole,—
> Imperfect qualities throughout creation
> Suggesting some one creature yet to make

....some point
Whereto those wandering rays should all converge |.|
["Paracelsus" V 681-92 (ms. text)]

This excerpt makes it clear that to Browning God was the Supreme Being. He also firmly believed in Truth and Love. It is quite evident in the character of Pauline. And in a close study of the poetry of Tagore we find that he also gave prime importance to God, Truth and Love. In the latter part of Tagore's life we see the predominance of divine thoughts and chanting of hymns to God. However, these two poets loved God in their individual ways and most probably did realise the ways of God and went deep into the mysteries of Creation.

Both Browning and Tagore had the firm conviction that God manifests Himself in all forms of nature and universe. Duffin maintains that to Browning "nature is God's temple, and the universe—felt and known, alive and sentient—is the Face of God" (202). And both of them were able "to enter into the varied life of the earth," which is a characteristic of the infinite lifespan of God. In this respect we are reminded of Browning's poem/ monologue "Mr. Sludge 'the Medium'" in which Sludge categorically emphasises his strong belief that "God is immanent in creation."

It is quite interesting to note that these two great poets viewed Nature as the divine manifestation of God. And Duffin maintains that "Browning feels that all nature conspires to speak to him of God; nature is God's temple, and the universe felt and known, alive and sentient—is the Face of God (or, as he said to Mrs. Orr, of Christ)" (202). And every human being is free enough to find God in his own way. This proposition is further strengthened by the sheer power of man's free will granted by God. Hence, each and every individual is separate, and is obviously guided by God; and naturally, each individual must be in quest of God in his own way. Again, Browning strongly believes that the earth is the testing ground and life on earth is essentially a probationary period, and thus is bound to be short and incomplete. But at the same time the poet emphasises that there remains the scope and provision for mending all sorts of shortcomings and incompleteness in the after-life. In heaven only we can achieve perfection and the pangs of failure on earth are replaced by success and eternal joy and immortality.

A careful study of the poems of Browning makes it clear that he had a strong and constant conviction in the compensation theory according to which the prospect of an after-life is always there to set right all the shortcomings of the mundane one. Duffin very critically points out the two-fold weakness of this compensation theory. He maintains: "The weakness of the compensation theory is, first, that it is built on the pusillanimous denial of life as good, and second, that it seems to represent God as having planned a bad world followed by a good one to atone for the first, which is uneconomic as well as inconsiderate" (213).

Thus it is quite evident that Browning did not entertain the concept of punishment—be it on the earth or in the heaven. His insistence on the love of God is best expressed in "The Last Ride Together," "Apparent Failure," and in "The Grammarian's Funeral." And it is the Grammarian who discards life and trusts death and strongly believes in "God's task to make the heavenly period perfect the earthen." This utterance of the Grammarian is equally true in the moral context of "Apparent Failure" which advocates a "second chance for those who have failed here." In other words, Browning considered 'the love of God as a guiding principle of creation." And Pippa is divinely inspired to utter:

> God's in his heaven —
> All's right with the World!

Incidentally, Tagore was very fond of the poem "Pippa Passes," and read it with his students at Santiniketan.

And in "La Saisiaz" the subject matter is the abstract theological question of the immortality of the soul. However, Browning affirms with no philosophical certainty but with somewhat illogical hope his belief in personal immortality. To say this is to underscore the view that Browning believed strongly in Soul and God.

Browning's poems, undoubtedly, highlight a philosophical urge/eagerness and complexity of mind. Naturally, in his poems Browning reflects, as Woolford and Karlin put, "the besetting problem of Western metaphysics...the conflict between monism and dualism (196). According to the famous exponents of monism there is no difference between a monist and a pantheist who believes that all material and spiritual things spring from a unified single universal substance. On the other hand, dualism claims that God is irreconcilable with matter and needs to be considered as, "the product of a different, 'higher' order of being." And only in the age of Romanticism we find the revival of monism prevalent in the form of a natural pantheism which binds together humanity with the natural world and with the divine order implicit in that world. According to the Philosophy of Romantic pantheism the universe which is quite visible to us is the body of God, and He is omnipresent in all things of the universe. This is the position explicitly stated at the end of "Paracelsus":

God tastes an infinite joy
In infinite ways—one everlasting bliss,
From whom all being emanates, all power
Proceeds; in whom is life for evermore,
Yet whom existence in its lowest form
Includes; where dwells enjoyment there is He!
....thus He dwells in all,
From life's minute beginnings, up at last
To man.... (V 628-33, 666-68).

Thus Paracelsus refutes his earlier claim that it is in the mind alone that "truth" resides, and Browning, through Paracelsus, endorses Romantic pantheism which categorically advocates God's incarnation and manifestation in the universe.

To elucidate the idea of God's incarnation as understood by Browning, we definitely have to follow what Woolford and Karlin observe while explaining "the Christian synthesis": "...Christ may be seen as a 'trope' through which the relation of the divine to the human, the infinite to the finite, is made humanly thinkable" (224). And the Christ metaphor signifies God's complete manifestation of His all—pervading love. Furthermore, in God's incarnation as Christ we find a marvellous synthesis of the material and divine elements of which humanity is made up.

Now it is quite surprising to see a strong similarity between Browning and Tagore on the point that both the poets were not philosophers in the traditional sense of the term. On philosophy Tagore observed that he would maintain a silence if the philosophical question of dualism or monism does surface. He only felt an immense joy of the manifestation of the God in himself. In Tagore we find the perfect fusion and unity of the objectives of philosophy and literature. He had a strong conviction that philosophy aims at surpassing the life of common men. He further realised that literature and philosophy in India are interrelated branches of study. In this respect we are gratefully reminded of S. Radhakrishnan's famous observation: "...though Tagore might not have a philosophy in the technical sense of the term he was the creator of philosophy of man and culture above all, in his quest of beauty and the meaning of art."

Thus it is widely known that though Tagore was not a Vaishnava, his concepts of the universe and life as reflected in his system of thoughts and vast range of literary creations amply suggest their similarities with the Vaishnava philosophical tenets. Especially, on the nature of the relations of universe, life and God Tagore's views are in consonance with those advanced by the philosophy of Ramanuja of middle age. In the words of Albert Scheweitzer: "Rabindranath Tagore is completing what Ramanuja undertook to do" (197). In addition to it, according to the view of R.C. Zachner the vision of Tagore is similar to that of Ramanuja. Tagore did not believe in Saṅkarācārya's concept of Adyaitabaāda. For, to him the idea of the existence of living beings not related to God and the very thought of God without His manifestations in all forms of life and universe—these two forms of higher thoughts are merely the distorted revelation of truth. N.K. Gupta, a critic on Tagore, thus, observes: "Nor does he discard the good things (preya) that earth and life offer to man for his banquet; and does not say like the base ascetic; "any avaco rimuncatha,"—"abandon everything else." But even like one of the Upanishadic Ṛṣis, the great Yājñavalkya, he would possess and enjoy his share of terrestrial as well as of spiritual wealth 'ubhayameva'" (200). And in the opinion of Zachner the first two verses of Isopaniṣadha "might serve as the text of which all the writings of Rabindranath Tagore are the commentary: they form the very stuff of his poetry" (188). Now, for developing a clear concept of these verses, we can consult S. Radhakrishnan's famous annotation: "The supreme is viewed not as the Absolute Brahman but as the cosmic Lord."

Thus we see that Tagore's philosophical conviction is primarily based on the Upanishadic sacred expression of "anðandam," and the simple belief of "baul" (Village bard). This is unequivocally evident in Tagore's view: "The Absolute is the Supreme Man, God humanised" (44).

Another aspect of Tagore's philosophy of life is universal humanitarianism which is a perfect synthesis of whatever is the best in art, religion, literature and culture of the East and West. To substantiate this point we may quote Prof. V. Lesny:

> The process of his development is in harmony with the tradition of Indian Philosophy: from insight into the beauty of nature he arrived at a feeling of confidence in the destiny of mankind; from a conviction of the nobility of man's mission in the world he derives a wise philosophy, which culminates in his unhesitatingly positive attitude towards life and in his later conception of the divine nature of mankind. He is not interested in heaven or celestial deities. It is in this world that man's progress towards perfection must take place, and therefore life in this world is the object of his pre-occupations.... Tagore's universal humanitarianism is the cornerstone of the collaboration between East and West... (6-7).

In one of his famous essays entitled "Personality" Tagore, quite in keeping with the tradition of ancient Indian Ṛṣis, beautifully analyses his concept of God:

> God with us is not a distant God; He belongs to our homes, as well as to our temples. We feel His nearness to us in all the human relationship of love and affection, and in our festivities. He is the chief guest whom we honour. In seasons of flowers and fruits, in the coming of the rain, in the fullness of the autumn, we see the hem of His mantle and hear His foot-steps. We worship Him in all the true objects of our worship and love Him wherever our love is true. In the woman who is good we feel Him, in the man who is true we know Him, in our children He is born again and again, the Eternal Child. Therefore, religious songs are our love songs... (358).

Tagore's "Song Offerings" is suffused with this feeling.

Both Browning and Tagore, though not without some differences of cultural and spiritual traditions they inherited, agree on the point of view of the visible world as the "vale of soul-making." The World, according to Browning, was created to be a place of trial, ordeal and probation. And there are various obstacles, limitations and uncongenial circumstances as well as antagonistic/ hostile forces which are unavoidable conditions of soul-development. But it is the supreme quality of love which brings about a communion between God and Man. Both the poets were keenly aware of the fact that God endowed man with will and resolution that can be occasionally tested. And in the absence of any clear prospect of eternity, the moral purpose of man's earthly life and the process of his soul-making in a finite world have not appeared to be impossible. Now we can safely observe that while Browning remained a Christian humanist, Tagore spread across the world his spiritual message of universal humanitarianism.

Apart from the concept of God's incarnation as Christ Browning's poetry does not offer any image of God's direct craving for meeting man in human embodiment. But in Tagore's poems, especially in the song offerings of *Gitanjali*, God is subdued with His overpowering desire to meet the devotee, their relationship appearing much in common with that of a pair of mortal lovers—both impatiently awaiting for a spiritual union. This

This poetic conceptualisation of God descending to His human devotee is quite unique and unprecedented. It also bears a mark of originality of the treatment of the theme of God-man relationship, and establishes Tagore's poetic faculties greater than those of Browning.

Browning's interest in matters of religion and also of irreligion is evident in his early Dramatic Lyrics and Romances, and in the plays. In all these writings the God's presence is seen everywhere in the World. It is Pippa who utters Browning's simple faith—"God's in his World." But in no poem composed before 1850 do we find Browning's preoccupation with the problems of Christian faith. He wrote "Christmas-Eve and Easter-Day" during the winter of 1849-50, and published it in April 1850. In the words of Gridley:

> 'The Christmas-Eve' section dramatises reactions to three modes of Christian worship: English Nonconformity as revealed during a service in a Dissenter Chapel in a London slum; Roman Catholicism (and by implication, High Anglicanism) as expressed in the rich pageantry of Mass in St Peter's in Rome; finally, we see a group of German rationalists in a Gottingen lecture hall trying to derive some sustenance from the husks of Christianity left to them after David Strauss's Hegelian analysis of the Myth of Christ had been perpetrated in 1835. The 'Easter-Day' section is a debate on 'How very hard it is to be/ A Christian' in the year 1850. The narrator examines the new philosophical, historical, geological and paleontological evidences until he spins 'dervish-like…through circling sciences,/ Philosophies, and histories!' Then, in a visionary trance, he affirms and submits to belief in a resurrected Christ (69).

The very idea of God's incarnation as Christ had a strong hold upon Browning's imagination and inspired some of the greatest poems of *Men and Women.* Thus the ideas of God's incarnation in Christ and Divine Love that man realises in his quest for God began to be reflected in Browning's religious poems and were never shaken throughout his life.

A number of other religious poems that Browning wrote in

the early 1850s were published in *Men and Women* of 1855. In this volume there are four major poems which have for their thematic preoccupation the specific contemporary spiritual unrest: "Saul," "An Epistle Containing the Strange Medical Experience of Karshish," "Cleon," and "Bishop Blougram's Apology." All these have a dramatic structure and have definite religious message voiced by sharply individualised speakers. "Saul" is spoken by David, "An Epistle" by an Arab Physician, "Cleon" has for its speaker a Greek Philosopher, and "Bishop Blougram" by a person reminding one of Cardinal Wiseman, who, in 1850, became Catholic Archbishop of Westminster. These poems exhibit many artistic aspects of Browning, and at the same time develop his religious attitudes of varying types.

"Cleon" is about immortality. "Apparent Failure" has for its theme the prospect of second chance and after-life for people who fail on the earth. The same idea is cherished by Andrea del Sarto, who fails to impress the world and with a bitter feeling comes to the conclusion at the end that God will compensate; again, the Grammarian has the strong conviction that God will definitely "make the heavenly period perfect the earthen," and unequivocally utters, "Give earth yourself, go up for gain above." In "Rabbi Ben Ezra" man's soul is conceived as a cup from which God "drinks the foaming wine of joy." Herein also we are enthused with the concept that life on earth is just a testing ground and death only prepares people for the after-life. All these poems predominatingly advocate what "Abt Vogler" has in its final part where Browning's conviction that the imperfections of this mundane life will be set right in the next one—"On earth the broken arcs; in heaven, the perfect round." The Grammarian also renounces life, trusts death and has an unflinching faith in "God's task to make the heavenly period perfect the earthen."

Tagore captures in his poems, much like the Vedic sages, the omnipresence of the all-pervading Almighty. He is the Supreme Poet or Artist—sometimes playing on his flute under the vast firmament while the sun, the stars and the planets seem to be His resplendent cows grazing in the skyscape, sometimes in the role of Shiva (Natarāj) in tune of whose dance rhythmically appear the human conditions of birth, death, joy and woe, laughter and tear. Yet underlying all these experiences run a strain of an inexplicable ecstasy. It is a pleasurable expression of creativity. Everywhere in nature and universe Tagore realises His presence. And it is man's meditative mind which experiences a deep and direct communion with God is one of the main propositions of Tagore's Pantheistic vision of God. His poetic mind also views God in different forms—beloved lady, wife, Eternal Child, friend, divine shepherd, Jibandevata, Jesus Christ, and Hindu gods and goddesses. This Supreme Power has a definite divine message for the entire mankind, and Tagore not only eagerly listens to it but also conveys it meaningfully to the people of the world. His song offerings are to God; the entire volume of *Gitanjali* and a few other reverberate with divine fervour and complete subjugation at His feet. Only through total dedication to God Tagore achieves spiritual union with Him and wishes his readers as well as everyman to do likewise for achieving self-realisation and enjoying the divine grace of the Almighty.

Victor Ivbulis, finds some critics not wrong to "think that the philosophical background of 'Jeevan-devatā' is the Vedantic idea about the Infinite Spirit being the single Ultimate Reality, the Supreme Soul pervading and permeating everything, finding its domicile, as it were, in the human soul and manifesting itself through it" (79). Obviously for this idea Tagore has an indebtedness to the Upanishads. To substantiate this Ivbulis quotes Tagore: "I feel my innermost God has a joy in expressing himself through me—this joy, this love pervades every part of my being, suffusing my mind, my intellect, this entire universe which is so vivid before me, my infinite past and my eternal destiny" (79).

However, it is evident from Tagore's poetry that his "Jeevan-devatā" is not God in a religious or philosophical sense although it appears to be so when Tagore offers the image of a Helmsman or the King of kings receiving his offerings. For example, in the poem "Jeevan-devatā" (The Deity of Life) a romantic heroine, presumably in love with the male of the poem, is seen offering her joys, painful experiences, weaving her bride-chamber with colourful things, fragrances, melodies and rhythms. Here 'the deity of life' is almost similar to the later concept/image of God of *Gitanjali*. In the poems of *Gitanjali* the poet himself dedicates to the Lord of Life all his artistic creations, his songs, and endeavours to sing his melodies. And Tagore's aspiration to attain spiritual perfection is the central message of the monologue "The Indwelling One" ("Antaryami," 1894).

Be it the concept of poetic imagination or inspiration or any divine imagination, Tagore's "Jeevan-devatā" has varying appearances before his poetic sensibilities. This is explicit in some of his famous and widely discussed monologues. In "The Golden Boat" ("Sonār Tari," 1892) and "A Voyage to Nowhere" ("Niruddeser Yātrā," 1894) the central image is of the Helmsman who appears as male and female respectively. And in keeping with their different physiological properties they perform different activities. The Helmsman of "The Golden Boat" appears in a lonely boat and takes away the golden harvest of the poet, but refuses to ferry the poet in the role of a sincere peasant reaping the crops, an agricultural process, which symbolically stands for the poet's deep meditation of the Almighty even though he is unavoidably surrounded by varied forms of imperfections of the world. Here Tagore's exclusively personal experience has a universal implication for Tagore himself believed and wrote:

> Man throughout his life cultivates crops. His life resembles an island—he is surrounded by the unknown. What is manifest is this field. When the time draws near, the surrounding water rises and the island gets ready to be submerged again in the unknown, he may load the worldly boat with the eternal effects of his lifelong works. The world will accept all, but if man asks to be carried along with it, the world says, where is the room for you? This life has been enjoyed and to square up accounts one has to hand over his ego to Death as its rental (Biswas 74-75).

The aesthetic character of the "Jeevan-devatā" is beautifully portrayed in three monologues of outstanding merit: "A Voyage to Nowhere" ("Niruddeser Yātrā"), "By the Ocean" ("Sindhu-Pāre"), and "Playmate" ("Lilā Sangin"). In "A Voyage to Nowhere" the unknown, foreign lady is the female Helmsman whom the poet addresses as "O, the beautiful!" ("he sundari!") and in response to whose invitation he undertakes a journey with her by boat westward over the sea at times perilous, at times calm. Again, in "By the Ocean" we notice a perfect blend of the beautiful and the divine in the character of the "Jeevan-devatā." She is a mysterious lady; veiling her face she appears on horseback and rouses the poet or the lyrical "I" from deep sleep and makes him so spell-bound that he mounts the other horse made of "the smoke from the cremation ground," and follows her horse almost in a hypnotic trance. At the end of a long journey they reach a marvellous and magnificent palace. Unlike the female Helmsman of "A Voyage to Nowhere," this veiled mysterious lady makes the really afraid poet sit beside her upon a little bed amidst royal ornamentations and decorations. Then an old brahmin, calculating the auspicious moment, solemnises their marriage. Now the speaker takes the soft, warm hand of the unknown lady to his own hand, cold as ice. This is followed by the lady's gradual disclosure of her real identity. And as she unveils herself, the poet-speaker astonishingly looks into her face and immediately falls at her feet for he has in his heart a deep reverence for and devotion of the "Jeevan-devatā," and with tears in the eyes, much surprisingly and ecstatically, he utters spontaneously: "You are also here 'Jeevan-devatā!'" And in the poem "Playmate" she assumes the role of a playmate of the poet. In his absence she cannot concentrate in her activities spread over the vast universe. She is elusive and the poet's beloved lady. Aesthetically he feels her to be the unrivalled paragon of beauty. She activates the poetic imagination in the poet, involves him in creative activities and when the poetic creation is finished she suddenly disappears leaving him alone. Now, in the evening of his life, Tagore has the greatest fortune to be reunited with her.

This exalts his poetic mind and he realises an ecstatic joy in communion with her.

All these poems on the concept of "Jeevan-devatā" show that Tagore, quite unconsciously, shared the tradition of the Iranian and Arab Sufi poets who developed the "idea of the Supreme Spirit as the Beloved One—the Ma'shuqah or the Beloved or Sweetheart of the Individual Soul as much as of the Entire World" (195). Thus the Muslim Sufi poetic concept of the Ma'shuq, as a young woman, is always the Passive Beloved whom the human soul pursues as the Active Lover or the Āshiq is integrally related to Rabindranath's concept of "Jeevan-devatā."

So far we have concentrated on Tagore's unflinching faith in the divine manifestation of God in all creations of the universe. But in the last phase of his life, Tagore gathered bitter experiences as he witnessed innocent people were inhumanly tortured and killed by the power-hungry politicians and imperialist forces. The oppressions and injustice on the downtrodden people or toiling masses vehemently shook at the base of his faith in the justice administered by God. In some poems he questioned God, in a direct address, if He is at all merciful to those who have put out the divine light and polluted the fresh air and global atmosphere in various ways. This question is explicit in the short divine lyric "Prasna" (A Question) clearly addressed to God. And perhaps it would not be quite irrelevant to presume that Tagore died broken-hearted at a time when the Second World War was going on and evil forces were out to destroy the fabric or texture of universal peace and sanctity of man's life on earth. This brings in its association the assumption that though he lost faith in the divine dispensation of God, he never desisted from emphasising the need to rise above narrow sectarian or religious dogmas and customs and to be imbibed with the true sense of humanism, obviously universal in its implication, which is the real religiosity in a man. This is the central message of his "Religion of Man."

E.D.H. Johnson in his famous essay entitled "Robert Browning's Pluralistic Universe: A Reading of *The Ring and the Book* directly quotes William James who, in his Gifford lectures on "The varieties of Religious Experience," maintained: "The obvious outcome of our total experience is that the world can be handled according to many systems of ideas, and is so handled by different men and will each time give some characteristic kind of profit, for which he cares, to the handler, while at the same time some other kind of profit has to be omitted or postponed."

Robert Browning conformed to such a view of the world. His early volumes of poetry *Pippa Passes, Dramatic Romances and Lyrics, Men and Women* and *Dramatic Personae*—amply prove this point. Again, in *The Ring and the Book* Browning's strange similarity with Jamesian view of pluralistic universe is quite explicitly discernible. In *Pippa Passes* and *The Ring and the Book* we meet a pluralistic universe where live people of all sorts and conditions, living in all ages and geographical territories, climates, etc. For Cleon, Karshish, and the Saint John of "A Death in the Desert" the problems advanced by the Christian revelation are totally separate and distinct, and each tries to make tryst with its mystery in his own way. Similarly, Fra Lippi, Sarto and the Pictor Ignotus have consciously judged the various forms of success or failure in artistic creations.

To substantiate the premise that Browning willingly adopted the Jamesian Pluralistic approach to each material is apparent in some analogies which he draws in the opening of the poem: "Each facet flash of the revolving year." Like James Browning also held the view that the individual engenders truths on the world, he does so by exerting his will by overpowering the evil and thus functions as "a redemptive agent in the cause of humanity." Both Browning and James shared the common background, and one is astonished to find that they were very much similar in their "treatment of the psychology of the religious experience." James' pluralism goes beyond the multi-levels of the phenomenal world and is stretched far to include the inference that this world of ours is only one among many and we live in a

Pluralistic Universe. Browning's "Rephan" and many other poems do confirm this assumption. In one of the oldest and beautiful cities of the East there, appeared, in antiquity, a stranger of extraordinary character. He was found to be fixedly staring at a certain star (Rephan) in the heavens. It was a meaningless curiosity that had urged him to wander and descend on earth among human beings. In the poem the strange wanderer from the star (Rephan), in perfect agreement with his friends' request, offers some account of his way of life before he came to earth. As regards varieties of religious experience we have Browning's dramatic poem "Caliban upon Setebos" which is obviously a satire on the anthropomorphic concept of God. Unlike the Christian belief that God made this world out of love, Caliban puts forward the opinion that Setebos created this world out of envy or spite. However, Browning is not critical of Caliban; he strongly disapproves certain primitive forms of religions which prevailed even in the 19th century and wishes us to adopt the religious belief of the God of Love—a theological view that is in sharp contrast with Caliban's crude theology that attributes to Setebos anger and envy.

Tagore was, in all probability, neither a follower of William James whose Gifford lectures are discussions on "The Varieties of Religious Experiences" and Pluralistic view of the Universe nor imitated Browning's categorical disapproval of certain primitive forms of religions that percolated in the 19th century England. But it is quite surprising to note that Tagore's ideas and opinions on the religion and universe are much similar to those advocated by James and Browning.

Tagore did not believe in idols and idolatry which had enormously perpetuated superstitions among the uneducated section of the people, and he, though steeped in the Upaniṣadic doctrines, did judiciously incorporate the Baul texts in his view of the world. To substantiate this point we can quote Sisir Kumar Das:

> Tagore was the first English-educated Indian to appropriate the Baul texts into his world-view. He did not

> consider the Baul thought either as contradictory to the Upaniṣadic doctrines or as a self-sufficient alternative to them. But he valourised its heretic character, its rejection of all institutional religions. This recognition of a folk world-view resistant to canonical texts and institutions, provided a fuller picture of Indian religious plurality, the co-existence of religious sects, distinctive by social stratification—brahmanical and non-brahmanical, elite and folk—as well (Das 3, 19).

Tagore had the belief in the Pluralistic Universe, and to him the Supreme Being is manifest in different forms and through all His creations. He is the preserver and destroyer; He relates the finite to the infinite, the temporal to the eternal. This view of Tagore, according to Ajit Kumar Chakraborty, is reflective of Darwin's theory of the distinctive feature of each cell in human body. In Tagore's consciousness the evolution of cosmos is the finest artistic design of the Supreme Being in whom there is the constant fusion of all lives and personalities casting off their worldly limitations. Innumerable heavenly bodies and an equally uncountable number of human beings with all their diversities of varied nature emanate from and ultimately return to Him. In other words, Tagore's grand pluralistic vision of the universe includes the entire mankind in the process of rectification of the shortcomings and moral lapses—for, each individual has his/her own role to help the blossoming of the Lotus of Bramha ("Bramha Kamal") through evolution. The advancement of our present civilisation is a continuous onward process and is adequately reflected in many articles and later poems of Tagore, and this suggests that Tagore was an optimist as well as a meliorist like James and Browning.

WORKS CITED

Biswas, Oneil. "The Tagorean Poetic As a Study in Aesthetic," *Rabindranath Tagore in Perspective. A Bunch of Essays* (Calcutta: Visva-Bharati, 1989) 74-75.

Chatterji, S.K. *World Literature and Tagore* (Santiniketan: Visva-Bharati, 1971) 195.

Duffin, H.C. *Amphibian: A Reconsideration of Browning* (Delhi: Doaba House) 202.

Ghosh, Sisir Kumar (ed.). *Angel of Surplus: Some Essays and Addresses on Aesthetics: Rabindranath Tagore*, Interoduction ix.

Gridley, Roy E. *Browning* (London: Routledge & Kegan Paul, 1972) 69.

Gupta, Nolinikanta. "Tagore—Poet and Seer," *Collected Works of N.K. Gupta*, Vol. 1, rpt. Pondicherry, 1979: 200.

Ivbulis, Victor. "Rabindranath Tagore's 'Jeevan-devatā,' The Artist's Personality in the Eyes of Romanticists," in *Rabindranath Tagore in Perspective : A Bunch of Essays*. Visva-Bharati, 1989.

Johnson, E.D.H. "Robert Browning's Pluralistic Universe: A Reading of *The Ring the Book*." University of Toronto, Quarterly, U.T. Press, 31 (1961) 20-41.

Scheweitzer, Albert. *Indian Thought and Its Development*, 197.

Sen, Sachin. *Rabindra Sāhityer Paricaya*, 1346 B.S. 6-7.

Tagore, Rabindranath. "The Religion of Man," Unwin Books, 1961.

Tagore, Rabindranath. *The English Writings of Rabindranath Tagore*, Vol. 2, 3 ed. Sisir Kumar Das, Sahitya Academi. (New Delhi: Pauls Press, 1996) 358.

Woolford, John and Karlin, Daniel. *Robert Browning* (New York: Longman, 1996) 196.

Zachner, R.C. *Hinduism*, 188.

17

Poe Indianised: From "To Helen" to "Banalatā Sen"

RAMA KUNDU

BAUDELAIRE'S DEVOTION to Poe has been proverbial; his nine long years of Poe translation into French is now common knowledge as well as his emphatic declaration,—"Edgar Poe, who isn't much in America, *must* become a great man in France" (Regan 64).

Such a vociferous claim for Poe may not have been made in India. But nevertheless Poe's influence has imperceptibly penetrated into works of various regional languages here, particularly in Bengali, since Bengal came earliest in touch with literature abroad. Jibananda Das, an exceptionally talented poet of Bengal, whose birth-centenary falls in February 1999, is a case in point.

Jibananda Das (1899-1954), fondly held in the two Bengals as the poet of *Rupasi Bangla*[1] (Beautiful Bengal) is, to many, a quintessentially Bengali poet. Yet his poems often carry echoes of familiar English texts and myths. "Banalatā Sen,"[2] the first poem of his volume of poems entitled *Banalatā Sen* (1942), happens to be the poet's most celebrated poem,[3] and one of his finest. It is interesting to note the striking resemblance between this poem and Edgar Allan Poe's "To Helen," the two masterpieces in two different traditions, each being a well-known and acclaimed piece in the respective canon. They show a remarkable affinity in theme, mood and poetic texture, which provokes exploration.

The two poems appear to depict similar experiences. Poe's

life (1809-1849) has been described as "a fantastic study in insecurity, frustration and failure" (M.R. Stern and S.L. Gross 83). Indeed, he was "doomed" as it were, "never to find an emotionally secure acceptance by others" (Stern and Gross 83). Once he found sympathy in Jane Stanard, the mother of a school chum. This lady is supposed to be the Helen of "To Helen." Though she passed away in 1824, the elation of the experience of finding sympathy at last remained a treasured memory with the homeless boy, orphaned early in life, and he recorded it in poetical form in 1831.

Jibananda Das, also a short-lived poet, (younger to Poe by ninety years), was a withdrawn and shy man who avoided public exposure and did not like that people should know or discuss his private life. So, little is known about the events and developments, personal or otherwise, of his life.[4] However, it is common knowledge now that Das was also a lonely soul, restless, though not in the turbulent way of Poe, but rather in the sad resigned way peculiar to an oriental. (Also both ended up in alienation and abnormal death.) "Banalatā Sen," Das's most popular poem, renders the speaker's mood of surprised joy at finding the woman of his dream at last, an experience similar to the one so ecstatically depicted by Poe in "To Helen."

Indeed, the way the two poets apprehend their experience, react to it, and grapple with the expression throws up significant parallels; this is discernible even in the phraseology, in turns of expression. One may reasonably assume that as a professor of English literature in a college Das had read Poe's poem. Reading the two poems together one gets the impression that Poe's poem had been operating on Das's mind as an artistic influence,—like the memory of a dream, at the time he composed his own poem.

Not that the later poem turns to be an exact transcription of the former. There are apparently subtle, fine differences, which, however, point to subtler, finer similarities. Das's is surely not a Bengali replica of the American poem. Das seems to have personalised Poe's ecstasy in "To Helen," and recreated it into an essentially indigenous poem in "Banalatā Sen." Without this complete personalisation and Indianisation the poem could not have such wide popular appeal here. Thus the perceptive reader is delighted to uncover and recognise the pattern of echoes and resonances of Poe's Helen in its transformed yet recognisable Indian sibling.

The two poems present two idealised women as they are perceived by the respective poets. In their attempt to find an appropriate correlative for this idealised perception both poets reach out to worlds of ancients, of myths, of legends. The name "Helen" is evocative of the past, being fraught with so many associations. It also stands for a paradigm,—an epitome of incomparable beauty, the idol of romantic imagination. The name "Banalatā Sen," though phonetically resonant of Poe's title, semantically suggests a different ideal of beauty. It is a simple name, though not a common one, at least by the standard of Das's contemporary Bengal. The name suggests the unnoticed beauty of a wild creeper, flourishing/ languishing alone outside the ken of mundane/ casual observers. At the same time, the surname "Sen" may be found vibrant with past associations. It evokes a historical period of Bengal, supposed to be its prosperous golden age, when Bengali navigators ruled the Bay of Bengal, the Indian Ocean, and the Arabian Sea; hints of navigation along this route are interspersed in the poem, particularly in 1.2 and 1.11. Thus the title in each poem calls back to the remote past of its poet's cultural heritage.

Again, Poe mentions the "Nicean barks of yore,"—ships heading for the ancient port of Nicaea in North West Asia Minor. In Das's poem the reader is invited to a glimpse of ships sailing across the nautical miles from the Ceylonese Seas to the Sea of Malaya.

In Poe's poem Helen is identified with those ancient ships that brought the "weary way-worn wanderer" back to his native shore. Thus Poe expresses his feeling of homecoming that Helen has given him at last after a long wearying journey through life. Das's poem is also about homecoming; it is the experience of a traveller who is also a navigator. Images of navigation and navigators are common in Das's poems which often switch between past and present with the ease of a dream. It is of course a metaphorical journey where the speaker imagines himself as trudging miles for long thousand years,[5] and also sailing vast nautical spaces along the coasts of big and small islands scattered over the seas of South-East Asia. It is a journey undertaken in the darkness of night over land and sea. It is also a journey from the present to the past along the ancient routes of history and legend, carrying the road-signs of ancient cities. Thus the sailor is also a traveller whose journey takes him further back into the obscure darkness of "Vidarva," an Indian city of the legendary past. The unceasing journey has left the sojourner "a tired Soul" amidst the "frothful fuming sea of life" until he meets Banalatā Sen who gives him a little respite and peace at last. Thus for both the poets the dream-girl connotes a feeling of homecoming and both render the homecoming in terms of navigating imager which refers to a long-lost world of the past, and, at the same time, sharply focuses the archetypal contrast between the weary sea-journey and a fascinating haven of peace. Helen and Banalatā mean for their poets this haven of peace, the homecoming.

The two poets mention their favourite name in a murmuring half-whisper as if in a dream. Poe opens his poem with the name that rings like an engrossed invocation running through three stanzas. Das closes each of the three stanzas with "Banalatā Sen" as the last word. Both seem to be fondly lisping a name that stirs a world of emotions for each. It stirs Poe to overflowing exuberance; it requires Das to pause a little after each mention, so deeply moved he is by the very name. [Dr. Sumita Chakrobarty points out Jibananda's preference for the particular name in his prose works and poetry, and traces this to some nostalgic memory of the poet's subdued teenage love for a quiet shy girl (53)].

Both correspond to the traditional ideal of woman as the quiet figure of peace who nourishes both the body and the mind of the male. Though Helen is a name with classic associations, it gets personalised in the context of Poe's poem and suggests other and opposite associations than "terrible beauty" and destruction. On the contrary, it is a quiet and soothing beauty that restores one to peace and contentment.

Both Helen and Banalatā are perceived as "gentle." Helen is likened to the ships that "gently" brought the weary sailor home. Her gentleness lulls the waves and spreads over them like a perfume. Cleopatra was supposed to have received Antony with a fleet whose sails were drenched in perfume. Banalatā emerges upon the "frothing sea of life" as a perfumed haven,—"Darucini dwip,"[6] a spicy island. Her gentleness is further brought out by the metaphor of bird's nest. She softly raises her eyes which like bird's nest, hold out the promise of peace, rest, warmth. Both the visions are simultaneously ecstasising and soothing, and an exceptional natural fragrance is made to endow them both, enhancing the idea of the excellent impact of ecstasy and peace combined. Thus Helen's beauty reacts upon Poe as the sight of home soothes and excites the weary sea-farer, and he identifies her with a fragrant ship that perfumes the entire course. Her "hyacinth" hair also suggests fragrant beauty. For Das, Banalatā is a lone fragrant island in the far-off seas, and he regards her with the elation of the long-lost sailor as he kens land after hopeless, desperate, weary miles in the frothing sea. This fragrance may also be considered in the light of its common association of sexual intimacy and fulfilment.

In the second stanza of Poe's poem the speaker imagines himself as the navigator who has to roam long on "desperate" seas (implying difficult and hopeless journeys). This exactly corresponds to the situation of Das's speaker, who identifies himself with the lost sailor of a wrecked ship in the distant seas. Thus both the visions appear as fascinating counterpoints to the troubles and anxieties of a turbulent life.

Helen's hair, face and water-nymph-like (Naiad) airs restore the poet's imagination to the mythic past of glorious Greece and grandiose Rome. In Das's poem similar suggestions of a mythic past undergo a process of complete Indianisation. A comparison of the details will prove the point. Helen's hair is compared to "hyacinth,"—a fragrant flower, pale or greenish; it is also an almost immortal water-plant, that can be revived even after long withering just by sprinkling water. Banalatā herself becomes a spicy island off the coasts of Java/Mauritius in the seas of South-East Asia; and the dead past gets revived in her hair. Her hair is dark, thick, long,—the common hair-shade and type of Indian girls. (Incidentally, thick, loose hair, whether hyacinth or dark, may have the same sexual overtones; association of sexual rousing with long loose hair is common in both the cultures.) The darkness of Banalatā's hair seems to the poet to be a glimpse of the accumulated darkness of the past, the darkness of a Bidisha night. Bidisha implies an ancient city of a supposedly golden age of India, now dead and gone. Its remoteness from the present is further enhanced by the darkness of night. Thus the metaphor of the dark night of Bidisha for Banalatā's hair calls up the mysterious, inscrutable beauty of someone who is almost as remote and mysterious as that long-lost city in darkness.

Again, Helen's "classic face" is appropriately evocative of the associations that are stirred by her name,—"the glory that was Greece/ And (also) the grandeur that was Rome." And Banalatā's face is described as the fine sculptural art of Sravasti; her face is moulded in the beautiful shape and curvature that was once the proud possession of the ancient city of Sravasti. In this way the poets' feeling of homecoming at the discovery of the dream-girl also involves a return to ancient memories of a mythical past, resplendently glamorous and fascinatingly mysterious owing to its distance from the mundane present. She stirs up for both memories of past lives and ages, bright and remote at the same time. She is, as it were, not subject to spatio-temporal limitations but belongs beyond time and space as she stirs dreams and associations that are deeply embedded in the racial unconscious.

Both poems end in darkness. Poe ends with reference to the Psyche myth. He envisions a dark night where Helen waits, like Psyche for Cupid, with a cute rose-tinted lamp under her window-niche.[7] Das has his first and last glimpse of Banalatā in darkness. The darkness—in contrast to garish daylight—is also another synonym for homecoming—carrying the promise of rest and oblivion. His poem ends with twilight that softly dissolves into darkness, when at the day's end the last light fades out from the kestrel's wings, and all activities come to a stop, all birds and rivers come home. Amidst this pervasive quietness and darkness there is only one light. It is not the soft shaded light from an agate lamp, but its source is the more homely yet more elusive chimerical glimmer of the glowworms.

The two poems end with the tranquil silence of the night. Poe closes his poem with the image of a night that covers all discordant notes and shades. Only the window-niche is illumined by a subdued light that trembles with soft love and expectation of fulfilment. It may be noted, however, that the sense of security has been undermined by the very allusion to the Psyche myth which carries suggestions of insecurity and transience, fears of which Poe could never really overcome. Critics commonly acknowledge "the psychological insecurity that was deep in Poe's nature" (*Literary History of the United States*, V. 1, 321).

Das, on the other hand, prefers to forget both past myths and present reality in order to seek one moment of epiphany when there will be nothing else but an all-drowning darkness and the soothing presence of Banalatā. But here also we have hints of transience. Birds' nest is built for only one season. Banalatā, who has nest-like eyes, gives him peace, but only for "du danda" ("just a little time"). The end-lines of the poem, alluding to rivers merging into sea under darkness, hint not only at the lovers' union but also the effacement to be brought about by death. Darkness governs Das's poem from beginning to end. The speaker as traveller journeys in darkness; he sees Banalatā first in darkness; at the end it is an all-covering darkness; but this darkness, unlike the previous ones of loneliness-indirection-obscurity, is full of peace and hope. Again, this peace implies death too. Perhaps the poets have felt that no peace in this mortal/ change-ridden world is permanent and only dark death can give the assurance of lasting peace. Thus, the darkness which rises to cover the dream-visions at the end, may be symptomatic of death as well.

Feminist criticism may find it rather unpalatable that the two visions of women projected in these poems should appear to correspond to the traditional/ patriarchal notion of woman as the subdued, gentle, passive figure of soft, comforting beauty. But they may also be considered as epitomising an eternal human quest for peace and fulfilment. Both the women figures thus finally emerge as visions characterised by a quality of remoteness and purity not obtainable in this mundane world, and more appropriate to the "holy land" (Poe), or to the invisible impalpable state of epiphany, far removed from life and light.

A modern talent, having access to the world heritage, is nourished by various traditions, indigenous and global. Das's absorbed reading of the English poetry, in particular, was noticeably reflected in his own poetry (For example, the unmistakable shadow of Hopkins's "The Starlight Night" in "Harinerā," of Yeats's "Ephemerā" in "Ābār Bachar Kuḍi Pare"). It is quite likely that Das has come across Poe's "To Helen." But that need not put one on the defensive (as some critics of Jibananda seem to be). It is quite natural that when a sensitive mind registers its impression of an experience it becomes part of his mind, and he does not know when it enters and moulds his expression itself. At most it may be called unconscious transcription. But actually it is not so much transcription as personalisation.

Again, intimate personal experience, intense and profound, may be the same across time and space. And thus, similar experiences, even at the distance of ages and continents may call up akin images to express itself. The sea and the haven are archetypal images rooted in the subconscious memory of a forgotten past of navigation-adventure-romance-grandeur-weariness-love. This may be rooted in the racial subconscious of the American settler, and it may also have roots in the psyche of Bengal which had, at one time in the past, a glorious tradition of navigation.

Again, a disturbed mind is naturally inclined to stretch back to the past rather than the present when it seeks an objective correlative for peace.

There was a further temperamental affinity between the two poets. Both the poems have the tenor of a dream; they transcribe visions, seen in a dream, as it were. And we know how both the poets were obsessed with the idea of "dream,"[8] and how this dream led them too often to exotic antiquity, to the legends, myths, or to history so remote as to attain a layer of mythical dust.

However, in the final analysis it may be admitted that, as Dr. Chakraborty rightly points out, Jibananda draws upon international sources and extracts the essence of the heritage, but almost always his poems are placed in the context of India,—its nature and life, past and present (52). Acknowledging the influence of a precursor does not necessarily diminish the stature of a particular poet or the preciousness of a particular text. Rather it remains an aesthetic pleasure to follow the echoes and reverberations of a previous text on a succeeding one and realise with delighted surprise how the later poet absorbs the earlier text, and recreates it in a fresh context, to achieve a unique artistic feat.

NOTES

1. *Rupasi Bangla* is the title of a volume of poems by Das which are exclusively engaged with the simple homely beauty of rural Bengal.
2. "Banalatā Sen" was composed and published in a magazine a few years before the publication of the volume.
3. The critic cannot explain the phenomenon that "a poet could be so famous just for one poem" (R. Samanta. *Jibananda Prativa*. Calcutta: Alfa Publishing Concern, 1972: 37).
4. Dr. Sumita Chakraborty's two books are exception among Bengali criticism of Jibananda, and provide valuable information and insight into his life and works.
   (i) Chakraborty, S. *Kabitār Antaranga Pāth*. Calcutta: Prama Prakashani, 1995.
   (ii) *Jibanāuda Samāj O Samakāl*. Calcutta: Sahityalok, 1987.
5. Dr. Chakraborty rightly maintains that these thousand years are not just thousand years by count, but a conglomeration of generations and centuries reflecting the continuity of the self through time and space (1995: 50).
6. "Qarucini Dwip" has also been traced to the heritage of the luxurious culture of the middle East which had once influenced Bengali poets (*e.g.* Satyendranath, Nazrul, Mohitlal, *et al.* to a considerable extent (Chakraborty 1995: 55).
7. Another poem of Jibananda—"*Mitabhāṣan*" (Banalatā Sen) echoes Poe's lines: "As I got spent up through roaming so many seas in darkness, I saw

you standing with an agate lamp, on the shore of death" (English paraphrase by the present writer).

Also a song by Tagore may be recalled in this context:

"It seemed as if I had covered an endless stretch in order to reach your door.... From afar I have seen a secret shaded lamp burning under your window-niche" ("Mane holo Jeno perye elem antabihin path..."; paraphrase by the writer).

8. "All that we see or seem/ Is but a dream within a dream"—Poe. "A Dream Within a Dream."

WORKS CITED

Baudelaire, Correspondence, V.1.; rpt. P.F. Quinn, "The French Response to Poe" *Poe* (Robert Regan Ed.) (N.J.: Prentice-Hall, 1967) 64.

Stern, M.L. and Gross, S.L. (eds.). *The American Romantics* (New Delhi: Light and Life Publications, 1975).

Thorp, W., Johnson, T.H., Canby, H.S. (eds.). *Literary History of the United States*, Vol.1 (N.Y.: The Macmillan Press, 1949).

APPENDIX

Banalatā Sen

—Jibananda Das

Hājār bachar dhare āmi path hãtitechi pṛthibīr pathe—
Singhal samudra theke nisither andhakāre Mālay sāgare
Anek ghurechi āmi—
Bimbisār Asoker dhūsar jagate sekhāne chilām āmi
Āro dūr andhakare Bidarbha nagare—
Āmi klānta prāṇ ek—
Caridike jībaner samudra saphen
Āmāre du danda santi diyechilo
Nātorer Banalatā Sen.

Cul tār kabekar Bidisar andhakār nisā
Mukh tār Srabastīr kārukārya.
Ati dūr samudrer pare
Hāl bhenge ye nābik hārāyeche disā—
Sabuj ghāser des yakhan se cokhe dekhe
Dārucini dvīper bhitare
Temani dekhechi tāre andhakāre—

Boleche se—etodin kothāy chilen?
Pākhīr nīḍer mato cokh tule
Nātorer Banalatā Sen.

Samasta diner seṣe sisirer sabder matan sandhyā āse.
Dānār raudrer gandha muche phele cil
P,thibir sab rang nibhe gele pāndulipi kare āyoyan
Takhan galper tare jonākīr range jhilmil.
Sab pākhi ghare āse—sab nadī—
Phurāy e jibaner sab lenden
Thāke àudhu andhakār, mukhomukhi basibār
Banalatā Sen.

To Helen

—Edgar Allan Poe

Helen, thy beauty is to me
    Like those Nicean barks of yore,
That gently, o'er a perfumed sea,
    The weary, way-worn wanderer bore
    To his own native shore.

On desperate seas long wont to roam,
    Thy hyacinth hair, thy classic face,
Thy Naiad airs have brought me home
    To the glory that was Greece
And the grandeur that was Rome.

Lo! In your brilliant window-niche
    How statue-like I see thee stand!
    The agate lamp within thy hand,
Ah! Psyche from the regions which
    Are Holy Land!

LIST OF CONTRIBUTORS

Amarnath Jha, Head of the Department of English, Mithila University, Darbhanga, Bihar.

Asha Choubey, Lecturer in English, Kanya Mahavidyalaya, Bareilly, Uttar Pradesh.

R.K. Mishra, Reader in English, D.A.V. College, Titilagarh, Orissa.

Alka Saxena, Lecturer in English, D.A.V. College, Kanpur, Uttar Pradesh.

Digambar Singh Dewari, Lecturer in English, S.N. College, Chota Udepur, Baroda, Gujarat.

P.C. Pradhan, Head, Department of English, Godavari Mahavidyalaya Banpur, Khurda, Orissa.

Ranjit Singh, Reader in English, Sarah Tucker College, Tirunelveli, Tamil Nadu.

Sumita Nasker, Lecturer in English, Calcutta University, Calcutta, Uttar Pradesh.

Ameena K. Ansari, Department of English, Jamia Millia Islamia, New Delhi.

Veena Nare, Department of English, Lokneta Vyankatrao Hiray Mahavidyalaya, Panchavati, Nasik, Maharashtra.

Basavaraj Naikar, Professor and Chairman, Department of Studies in English, Karnataka University, Dharwad, Karnataka.

M.A. Nare, Department of English, Government Postgraduate College, V.M.V. Amaravati, Madhya Pradesh.

Stella, Department of English, Sarah Tucker College, Perumalpuram, Tamil Nadu.

Jayanta Bhattacharya, Research Scholar, Department of English, Burdwan University, Burdwan, West Bengal.

Rama Kundu, Professor of English, Burdwan University, Burdwan, West Bengal.